Ancient Peoples and Places

CENTRAL ASIA
Turkmenia before the Achaemenids

General Editor

DR. GLYN DANIEL

ABOUT THE AUTHORS

Professor V. M. Masson studied in the Department of Archaeology at the Central Asian State University, graduating in 1950. From 1951 to 1954 he continued his studies at the Leningrad Division of the Institute of Archaeology, USSR Academy of Science. In 1957 he was appointed lecturer in the Archaeology of Central Asia and the Ancient East at Leningrad University; since 1968 he has been head of the Central Asia and Caucasus section of the Leningrad Division of the Institute of Archaeology. V. I. Sarianidi, also a graduate of the Central Asian State University, worked for some time at the Samarkand Museum before becoming Senior Researcher at the Institute of Archaeology in Moscow. Both Masson and Sarianidi have taken part in excavations in Central Asia for over twenty years, specializing in Turkmenia and Afghanistan, respectively. They are the authors of numerous books and articles in their field.

CENTRAL ASIA

TURKMENIA BEFORE THE ACHAEMENIDS

V. M. Masson and V. I. Sarianidi
Translated and edited with a preface
by Ruth Tringham

53 PHOTOGRAPHS
43 LINE DRAWINGS
3 MAPS

PRAEGER PUBLISHERS
New York · Washington

THIS IS VOLUME SEVENTY-NINE IN THE SERIES

Ancient Peoples and Places

GENERAL EDITOR: DR. GLYN DANIEL

BOOKS THAT MATTER

Published in the United States of America in 1972
by Praeger Publishers Inc.,
111 Fourth Avenue, New York, N.Y. 10003

ⓒ1972 in London, England, by Thames and Hudson Ltd.

Library of Congress Catalog Card Number: 70–131350

Printed in Great Britain

CONTENTS

List of Illustrations

8

Translator's Preface

This book comprises the first synthesis of the prehistory of that part of the USSR which is referred to as Central Asia to be written by a Soviet archaeologist in the English language. It is written by two of the foremost prehistorians specializing in this area, both of whom have been responsible for the excavation of sites which have proved crucial in building up information on the beginning of agriculture and the rise of urbanization in this northern outpost of the Near East.

Central Asia will be published first in this English translation; it has not yet been published in the USSR. The preliminary arrangements for its publication were made during a visit by Professor Stuart Piggott and myself to Moscow and Leningrad in the summer of 1968. Perhaps as a result of my early association with the book, as well as my personal interest in the prehistory of the USSR, I was asked by the publishers to assist in the editing of the text and to take over its translation, whose preliminary stages had already been carried out by Novosti Press in Moscow.

Apart from general editing, including the removal of certain bibliographical references which would be unavailable to the general English-speaking reader, my aim was to ensure that the concepts and material evidence of my colleagues, Drs Masson and Sarianidi, should be expressed as accurately as possible. Certain terms, in particular geographical terms and place-names, have been anglicized for obvious reasons, but this was kept to a minimum.

I should like to express my deep admiration for the book and my thanks to Drs Masson and Sarianidi for the pleasure they have given me in allowing me to render their very fine work into English.

RUTH TRINGHAM

CHAPTER I

Background

Europeans first learnt of Western Central Asia and its people in con- nection with the campaigns undertaken by Darius and Xerxes against the freedom-loving Hellenic towns in the fifth century BC: Asian troops and horsemen in the Persian army fought at Marathon, Thermo- pylae and Plataea. This was the first mention of a distant and enigmatic country which from then on appeared more and more often in historical records. It was the Asian Sogdianians who valiantly resisted Alexander the Great, and it was from Western Central Asia that he took his beautiful wife. This part of Asia played no small part in the formation of the Parthian state and the Kushan Empire, two great powers of the ancient world. However, as archaeological excavations have revealed, the prehistory of Western Central Asia dates back thousands of years. This is a land of long vanished civilizations, of alternating prosperity and stagnation. One of the first archaeological expeditions here was led by governor-general A. V. Komarov, who in the early 1880's opened up two mounds near the village of Anau, a short distance from Ash- khabad. It turned out that these two seemingly nondescript humps of earth, lost in the boundless Kara Kum Desert, contained the remnants of an ancient culture. The surface excavation made by A. V. Komarov attracted a group of American archaeologists under R. Pumpelly to these parts. The Americans carried out some additional excavations in 1904 and later published their findings in two large volumes. Since that time the village of Anau has held an important place in studies of the Ancient East.

Later studies showed that the mounds of Anau were all that remained of the settlements which had once stood alongside large prosperous centres. Of these, the most important was Namazga-depe where extensive excavations were carried out by B. A. Kuftin in 1952. At the same time systematic studies and excavations led to the discovery of many more prehistoric sites and cultures in other areas of Western Central Asia. It seems that the Achaemenian 'kings of kings' found an advanced stage of civilization here and that the local cultures had at one time reached a surprisingly high level. Recent discoveries have thrown additional light on the past of this part of Asia within the history of the Asian continent and the Old World as a whole.

TOPOGRAPHY

These relationships were to a great extent determined by the geographical position of this land-locked country lost in the interior of the Asian continent. The two large deserts, the Kara Kum and the Kysyl Kum, comprise most of its plateaux. The undulating sandy relief, scanty rainfall, cold winters and hot summers, when the temperature of the sand rises to 79° C, are common to both deserts. At the same time the grass that grows in the sand, and particularly on the barren steppes, provides a sufficient source of food for hardy breeds of sheep and goats. In this respect the lowlands of Western Central Asia, and particularly the northern lowlands, are linked with the vast Asian steppe, which from early times has been known for its cattle-breeders and nomadic cultures.

The most suitable areas for early agriculture were submontane plains; these were covered with fertile loess and, because of their proximity to the mountains, were more temperate in climate and had more rainfall than elsewhere in the desert. Although they were not as rich and fertile as the subtropics, where many of the early civilizations made their appearance, geographical conditions in the south-western part of Asia are in many ways similar to those in the Near East. The Kopet Dag is part of the Turkmeno-Khorasan mountains, the northern edge of which forms the boundary of the Kara Kum Desert. At a relatively low level (up to 3,300 m. above sea level), these mountains merge with the Elbruz range in the west and with the Parapamir in the east, thus forming the northern frontier of the Iranian plateau. The plant and animal life, too, of the Kopet Dag is similar to that of the Near East, in particular Iran.

In other parts of Western Central Asia conditions are more difficult for land cultivation than in the submontane area. But with artificial irrigation the fertile loess soil of the Fergana Valley and the basin of the Chirchik, Zeravshan and Kashak Darya rivers yield excellent harvests.

The Amu Darya and the Syr Darya merit special attention as the two main waterways of the country. Being limited to enclosed inland basins, they were of little importance as trade routes and barely influenced inter-tribal relations. Even when water flowed from the Amu Darya into the Caspian Sea, down the Uzboi, which was undoubtedly the case in the

Mesolithic and Neolithic periods, it was still essentially the same enclosed inland basin, albeit of giant proportions. The difficulty of bringing water to the fields from the main channel of the Amu Darya explains the fact that agriculture in this area first appeared only in its delta. The rigorous climatic conditions in the Syr Darya delta, however, prevented it from ever becoming an important agricultural area. As a result, in the early stages of its development, Western Central Asian civilization was centred on small oases rather than large rivers.

The Pamir plateau, of considerable importance, resembles a miniature Tibet, and its animal life includes many species of Tibetan fauna. Here, even the valleys lie at an altitude of 3,600–4,000 m. above sea level, while the mountain ranges and occasional peaks reach 5,000–7,000 m. The dry, cold climate and sparse vegetation make the Pamir a kind of highland desert. A country of hunters and cattle-breeders, the Pamir forms a bridge between this part of Asia and the Tibet-Indostani world, in the same way as the Kopet Dag of Turkmenistan links Western Central Asia with the Near East.

CHAPTER II
The Old Stone Age

Western Central Asia has not yet yielded any finds relating to such an early stage in the history of mankind as have recently been found in East Africa. What is more, its environmental conditions in the Pleistocene period raise doubts that it was ever part of the hominid zone. By the end of the Tertiary period the area developed a dry continental climate and mixed desert-steppe, very much the same as today.

During the Quartenary period, Western Central Asia was not covered by an ice-sheet comparable to that in Europe and North America. Glaciers lay predominently in valleys and their activity was limited mainly to mountainous areas. On the plains, the cold rainy periods were associated with intense fluvial activity and with a substantial rise of the Caspian Sea.[1] With the onset of cold temperatures Western Central Asia was invaded by northern peri-glacial fauna. For example, mammoth bones have been found in the Fergana Valley and near Alma Ata, and the remains of woolly rhinoceros have been discovered near Tashkent and in a number of places in the Tien-Shen mountains.

THE LOWER PALAEOLITHIC

Occasional dissociated finds prove that the first groups of people appeared in Western Central Asia at the time of the Lower Palaeolithic and that human settlement spread there from different directions. The peculiarity of the Palaeolithic of south-east Asia, where assemblages with pebble-tools occur, has for a long time aroused the keen interest of archaeologists. Although recent evidence points to the co-existence of tools made of pebbles and by non-pebble technology, the predominance of the first type in a number of assemblages is obvious.

In the eastern parts of the area a large number of finds (among them a hand-axe and a skin-scraper at the village of On-archa in the Tien-Shen mountains) testifies to the presence of a rather primitive pebble-tool industry. Pebble-tools have also been found in several other sites of the Tien-Shen mountains and the Fergana Valley. At the foot of the Little Karatau, in southern Kazakhstan, a number of artifacts of the lower Palaeolithic period have been recovered. These include a wide variety of crudely-made chopping tools, nondescript cleavers and amorphous cores (Borikazgan, Tanirkazgan). Researchers date the early Karatau artifacts to the Chellean-Acheulian period. Both culturally and historically these complexes and individual artifacts are connected more with the zone of pebble-tools in south-eastern Asia and northern Indostan. Possibly the direction of this cultural diffusion reflects to a great extent the direction of expansion of human settlement to these areas by mountain hunters during the Lower Palaeolithic period. At any rate, it was here, in the mountain areas of Western Central Asia, that the local traditions of the pebble industry had a marked influence on the subsequent periods of the Stone Age.

At the same time, on the basis of occasional significant finds, the western parts of the areas adjacent to the Caspian Sea were connected to the Near East and the Caucasus in the general form and content of their material culture. For example, Acheulian traditions are apparent in artifacts found on the Krasnovodsk peninsula, the Mangishlak peninsula and the lowlands of Kazakhstan.

Fig. 1

THE MOUSTERIAN PERIOD

The predominance of this western tradition in most of the known Western Central Asian complexes of the Mousterian period is an indisputable fact. On the whole the number of Mousterian sites is small in proportion to the vast territory of the region; they include open camp-sites, cave-dwellings and ancient quarries.

The first Mousterian complex was discovered in the cave of Teshik-tash, where in 1938–39 rich Palaeolithic material, including the burial of a Neanderthal boy, was found. This cave is situated in southern Uzbekistan, in a spur of the Hissar Range, at an altitude of 1,500 m. The cultural layer is about 1.5 m. thick and divided into five levels. However, the material obtained at Teshik-tash shows that the culture of these five levels belongs to just one industry. All the tools were fashioned out of quartzitic limestone, which would account for the crudity of the artifacts. These undoubtedly belong to the Mousterian industry, and include typical artifacts of that period such as discoidal cores, pointed flint tools and scrapers. Some of the pointed tools are triangular in outline, with one side concave and the other convex. The split bones, used as anvils, show that the tools were made in the cave.

Plate 1

Fig. 1 Chipped stone industry of the Lower (a, b) and Middle (c–e) Palaeolithic of Central Asia. a On-archa; b Krasnovodsk; c Obi Rakhmat, d Kara-Bura; e Teshik-tash. Approx. 1:3

The flesh of killed animals was also brought to the cave. Judging by the osteological material, the Siberian mountain goat predominated in the diet of the Teshik-tash hunters. Of the 907 bones found here, 761 belong to 38 mountain goats. There are also bones of deer, horse, leopard, bear, hare, small rodents and birds. The composition of the fauna was typical of high mountains and differed very little from that of the present day. The climatic constancy of the natural environment is borne out by the presence of carbonized juniper in the ashes of a camp-fire—this tree still grows here in the mountains, at the same altitude as the Teshik-tash cave. All this points to the fact that the Mousterian complex of Teshik-tash dates to an interpluvial/interglacial period. At first Soviet researchers dated the finds of the Teshik-tash cave to the Mindel-Riss interglacial period, but now they tend to believe that the Teshik-tash complex is of much more recent origin.

Another cave, the Amir Temir Grotto, situated nearby, has yielded a comparatively small number of Mousterian scrapers and cores, as well as bones of mountain goat, all lodged in its bottom layer. Evidently prehistoric man visited this low, damp grotto only occasionally, and the same would seem to be true of the low karst Aman Kutan cave, about 43 km. south of Samarkand, which has yielded very few finished tools. At the same time, judging by such artifacts as a discoidal core, scrapers and points, all the finds in this cave are within the Teshik-tash cultural range. The fauna of Aman Kutan is worth noting. Just as in Teshik-tash it is practically the same as that of the present day, but represents a different altitude zone—that of foot-hills and plains. Mountain goats are completely absent, but a large number of sheep

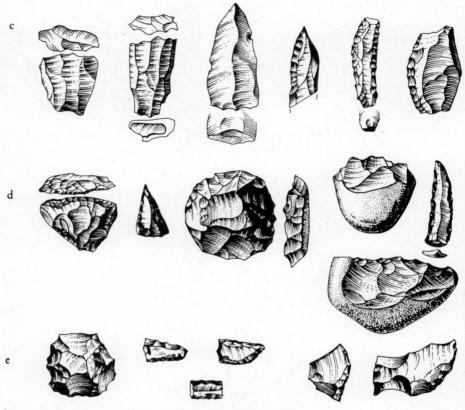

c

d

e

bones were found which have been identified as belonging to 116 individual animals. In addition deer, roe and onager were found among the skeletal remains of this cave, including the bones of 39 brown bears. Turtle held a prominent place in the diet of the Aman Kutan inhabitants.

Over the past few years excavations have been made in several caves with Mousterian cultural layers along the River Chirchik north-east of Tashkent. Prominent among these are the Khodjakent 1 and Khodjakent 2 caves, where, just as in the Teshik-tash, campfire ashes and bones of mountain goat have been found. In addition to typical Mousterian discoidal cores, cores with one or two surfaces, long flint blades and a very large pointed flake tool were found here.

CASPIAN
SEA

ARAL
SEA

▲ Kavat 5
▲ Djanbas-kala

Amu Darya

▲ Gavlake
▲ Besh-Bu

Dam-Dam-Chashma
Djebel

▲ Turkan

○ Bami
Chopan-depe
○ ○ Djeitun

Tes

○ Chakmakli-depe

- • Palaeolithic sites
- ▬ Mesolithic sites
- ▲ Neolithic sites
- ○ Villages of the Djeitun culture

Fig. 2   The distribution of Stone Age sites in Central Asia

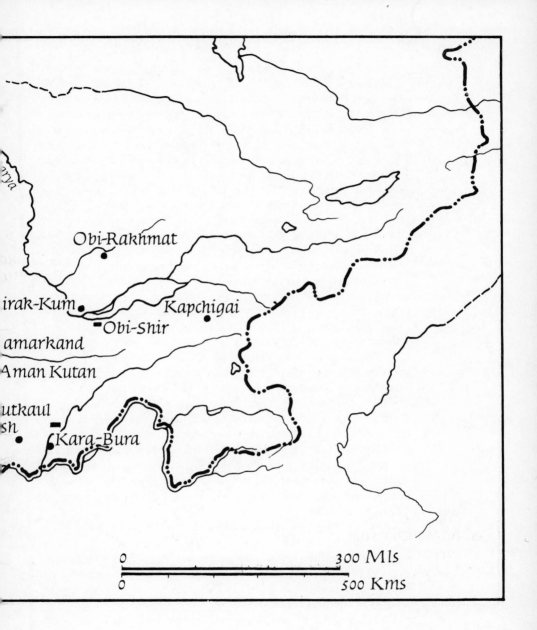

arya

Obi-Rakhmat

irak-Kum

Obi-Shir

Kapchigai

amarkand

Aman Kutan

utkaul
sh

Kara-Bura

```
0                        300 Mls
0                        500 Kms
```

19

One of the most important Palaeolithic assemblages of Western Central Asia is that from the Obi-Rakhmat cave, situated 100 km. north-east of Tashkent. This spacious, dry cave served for a long time as a shelter for Palaeolithic hunters: altogether twenty-one Palaeolithic layers 10 m. thick have been found here. The cave has ample skeletal remains of killed game, mostly Siberian goat, deer and sheep, as well as porcupine, boar and cave lion. The gradual evolution of the Obi-Rakhmat flint industry is of great interest. The lower layers of the cave represent the Mousterian complex of Teshik-tash type with its discoidal cores, the number of which, however, is small. With time these were replaced by cores of proto-prismatic and prismatic forms. The tools of later periods included large blades, with retouched distal ends, while scrapers of archaic shapes gradually disappeared and gave way to knives. An increasing number of tools were made on blades, similar to some of the better known Near Eastern industries of pre-Aurignacian-Amudien type. It is quite possible that the later deposits of Obi-Rakhmat were among the oldest Upper Palaeolithic assemblages of Western Central Asia. The material of Obi-Rakhmat gives a good idea of how this industry was formed on the basis of the Mousterian Teshik-tash industry.

Still more numerous in Western Central Asia are open camp-sites of the Mousterian period. No cultural layers have been preserved at these sites. They are represented only by stone tools, either as stray finds or as fairly large assemblages.[2] Finds such as these, which occur right on the Caspian coast, together with the cave-assemblages, show that Mousterian man lived in almost all natural environments.

At Kairak-Kum, on the bank of the Syr Darya, between Naukat and Leninabad, artifacts were collected from old, largely obliterated, terraces, including discoidal cores and scrapers, points, and occasional narrow long blades reminiscent of the blades from the upper layer of Teshik-tash.

Material recovered at the Kara-Bura site, in the valley of the River Vakhsh, is also very rich. It includes discoidal uni-facial and bi-facial cores, with a smaller number of points and scrapers, and, most important, numerous artifacts recalling pebble cultural traditions—hand-axes, chopping tools and pebble cores. The entire complex resembles late Soan-B in northern Hindustan.

This mass of stone tools, which has become the object of a detailed study, required a great deal of raw material for their manufacture. After years of research, archaeologists discovered several Mousterian quarries. Two of them—Uchtut and Idjont—are situated on the spurs of the Karatau mountains, in the middle course of the Syr Darya, and the other two—Okhna and Kapchigai—are near the town of Fergana, in the Fergana Valley. In Kapchigai, the flint was quarried directly from the cliffs, from layers 2–3 m. thick, and the tools used for mining and shaping the implements were made from large fragments of the same flint. The discovery of cores, blades, several points and scrapers indicates that the manufacture of tools was carried out partially near the rich flint outcrops on the banks of an ancient river tributary which once flowed here.

All these sites—caves, camps and quarries—have yielded rich material relating to Western Central Asia in the Mousterian period; high priority has been given to the problem of spatial and chronological classification. When the first descriptions of the Teshik-tash finds were released A. P. Okladnikov pointed out their similarity to the artifacts from the Near East, especially from Palestine. Recently, however, especially after the publication of the works of F. Bordes, Mousterian scholars have identified many distinct local variants or cultures which co-existed at that time. For example, V. A. Ranov proposed the following divisions: Levallois-Moustier, Alpine Moustier (Teshik-tash) and the Mousterian Soan (Kara-Bura). He distinguished two basic techniques in the first group—Levallois industry (Khodjakent, Obi-Rakhmat) and Levallois-Mousterian industry (Kairak-Kum, Kapchigai, and South Fergana). An exhaustive study of local cultural distinctions was made by R. H. Suleimanov. He pointed out that at many sites in Western Central Asia, and particularly in the Obi-Rakhmat cave, Levallois flakes accounted for not more than 30% of the total artifacts, which makes it impossible to consider it of basically Levallois origin in the sense of the term used by Bordes. Suleimanov argues that the material from Teshik-tash, Khodjakent and Obi-Rakhmat, Kairak-Kum and South Fergana comes from one local Mousterian cultural source, which he suggests should be called the Obi-Rakhmat culture, with Teshik-tash at the top and Obi-Rakhmat at the bottom of the chronological scale. A number of sites in the middle course of the River Zeravshan, which demonstrate the genuine Levallois technique, and the village of Kulbulak near Tashkent are outside the mainstream of this culture. The Levallois technique is also typical of some sites on the Mangishlak peninsula.

With all this diversity of cultures Western Central Asia in the Mousterian period should still be regarded as a single geographical entity; hunting was the main source of food everywhere. Under the typological classification of Bordes, about 60 varieties of Mousterian tools have been established, many of which have different functions. A certain degree of specialization of hunting communities in Western Central Asia (Teshik-tash: Siberian goat; Aman Kutan: sheep and bear), shows the high level of skill of the hunters and their excellent knowledge of the game. All this enabled the community to stay in one place for many months, provided they found suitable shelter. Evidence of this is the thick Mousterian strata in the caves of the Near East, an example of which is Obi-Rakhmat in Western Central Asia. These were a specific kind of cave settlement where campfires were maintained, food was cooked, tools were made and animal skins were processed.

Important evidence of the high level of development of Middle Palaeolithic man is found in the Mousterian burials. Of these the grave of a Neanderthal boy aged 8 or 9 at Teshik-tash merits special attention. It was lined with the horns of mountain goat, which were inserted in the ground, showing that the burial was not accidental and that a certain funeral ritual had been observed. At the same time the choice of animal is also rather significant. The mountain goat was the basic and almost exclusive animal hunted by the Teshik-tash community. The inclusion of the horns of this particular animal in the magic ritual points to the existence of emergent totemism. This new religious concept has its analogy in the bear cult which loomed large in the European Mousterian. Thus we are dealing here not only with a food-gathering economy at its highest level, but also with the beginnings of an associated ideology.

It is quite possible that a number of progressive features in the structure of the Teshik-tash boy's skull point to the incipient evolution of Neanderthal man towards the ancestors of modern Man.

THE UPPER PALAEOLITHIC

The Upper Palaeolithic sites of Western Central Asia found so far are neither so numerous nor so characteristic as the open sites and caves of the Mousterian. Except for a camp-site near Samarkand, all this material

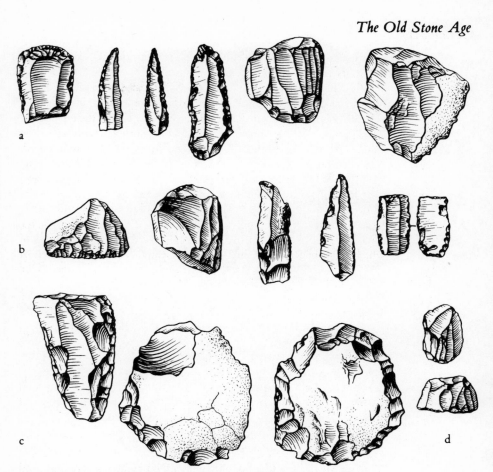

*Fig. 3 Chipped stone industry of the Upper Palaeolithic period. a Hodji Gor;
b Turkmenia; c Samarkand site; d Kisil Kala*

comes from scattered settlements and from stray finds. Nevertheless,
they give a full enough picture of the general cultural aspect of the
Upper Palaeolithic period of Western Central Asia. As in the Near
East the Aurignacioid features of the flint industry are very pronounced.

One of the earliest Upper Palaeolithic sites of Western Central Asia
was found 39 km. east of Krasnovodsk. Judging by the high concentra‑

Fig. 3

23

tion of finds in a small area, the site once served as a kind of Upper Palaeo-lithic workshop. Apart from a few discoidal examples, the cores found here were predominantly prismatoid in shape. The development of purely Upper Palaeolithic techniques is apparent in the presence of regular blades with very precise faceting which were used as blanks for scrapers and piercers. Scrapers were also made on cores. The fact that assemblages of this type are widespread in Western Central Asia is borne out by the discovery of a backed scraper near the village of Kisil Kala, in the valley of the River Vakhsh. This tool looks very much like one from the Aurignacian complex in the cave of Kara Kamar, in northern Afghanistan. It has been dated to about 25–34 thousand years ago which coincides in time with the radio carbon chronology of the Upper Palaeolithic period in the Near East. During the Upper Palaeo-lithic period the quarries of Kapchigai (in the Fergana Valley), Uchtut and Idjont, in the middle course of the River Zeravshan, were still used. Prismatic cores, flakes and scrapers, all of which were very common in that period, were found here. Recently, excavations were begun on the Kulbulak site, near Tashkent, where two Upper Palaeolithic levels were discovered, with remains of camp-fires in them, immediately above the Mousterian deposits.

The best-studied Upper Palaeolithic site—the Samarkand camp-site, with its magnificently preserved cultural layers, was found within the confines of a park in Samarkand. Three cultural layers were excavated, separated by sterile layers. The remains of camp fires were preserved and the high concentration of artifacts in certain places seemed to point to the presence of temporary dwellings. The excavation revealed deer antlers stacked in neat piles. Tools were made at the site itself; the flint tools found here retained many archaic features and do not belong to the Aurignacian industry. The cores are mostly discoidal, although their number also includes roughly prismatic and bi-facial examples. Points also occur, and very characteristic massive shavers of core shape, also thin blades of regular shape, thick notched blades, knives, pointed scrapers made out of flint flakes, and roughly-hewn chopping tools. The Samarkand camp-site undoubtedly holds an unusual position among the other Upper Palaeolithic sites, although its exact relationship with other settlements of this period has not yet been established.[3] It appears that the economy of this Palaeolithic community was based on food-gathering. The population consisted primarily of hunters, whose principal game was wild horse, (which resembled the Przewalski horse), the Pleistocene donkey, and more rarely camel, aurochs and bison. Bones of sheep and saiga were also found. The tools recovered here were not only used for obtaining and processing food; chopping tools like the axe, for example, could be used for building light frame houses, while pounders made out of coarse granite were used for fragmentation of ochre, which was the favourite pigment of Upper Palaeolithic man. In-cidentally, the human jaw found on the Samarkand site belongs to a man of clearly modern type.

It seems that the Hodji Gor complex in north-western Tadjikistan represents the final phase of the Upper Palaeolithic period. Excavations here produced many well-preserved prismatic cores, thin blades, small discoidal flake scrapers, Gravettian points, but not a single geometric microlith. The sophisticated blade-working technique evidenced by the Hodji Gor material was among the highest achievements of Palaeolithic man; the comparative ease with which it enabled large quantities of tools to be made was one of the most important factors in the further economic progress which continued during the next, essentially transitional period known as the Mesolithic.

CHAPTER III

Mesolithic Ancestors

In the highly developed areas of the Old World the Mesolithic period linked two great epochs in the history of man: the period of a food-gathering economy and the period of a production economy. Recent archaeological evidence indicates that it was during the Mesolithic period that the domestication of animals was begun, and that it is most likely that at that time the first attempts were made to grow cereal crops. All this has encouraged the use of such terms as 'Protoneolithic', 'Pre-ceramic Neolithic', etc. It seems, however, that these substitutes for the traditional and in many cases rather convenient terminology are by no means always the most rational when it comes to historical periodization. Until another system of archaeological classification has been devised, there-fore, the term 'Mesolithic' would seem to be convenient enough to suit our purpose.

Mesolithic Western Central Asia, as in the Palaeolithic period, presents a very variegated ethnical picture. The majority of the Mesolithic groups that developed a distinctly blade-type industry, microlithic techniques, and tools of geometric shapes, resemble closely the Mediter-ranean culture complex, the aggregate elements of which are designated 'the Capsian tradition'. At present three groups of sites belonging to this tradition are known in Western Central Asia, which are likely to correspond to three cultures of the Mesolithic period.

THE CASPIAN SEA GROUP

Fig. 4

The best known of these are the sites of the Caspian Sea group, which are represented by the caves of Djebel, Dam-Dam-Chashma 1 and Dam-Dam-Chashma 2 in the Balkhan mountains and by the Kailiu grotto on the Krasnovodsk peninsula.[1] The northerly spread of sites of this type is seen in the Late Mesolithic site of Hodja-Su I on the eastern coast of Kara Bogaz.

Among the earliest artifacts found on the Caspian shore are the flint implements from the Dam-Dam-Chashma 1 cave. These include piercers, pointed scrapers, backed blades and lunates. On the other hand the geometric tools found in the Early Mesolithic layers (6–7) of the

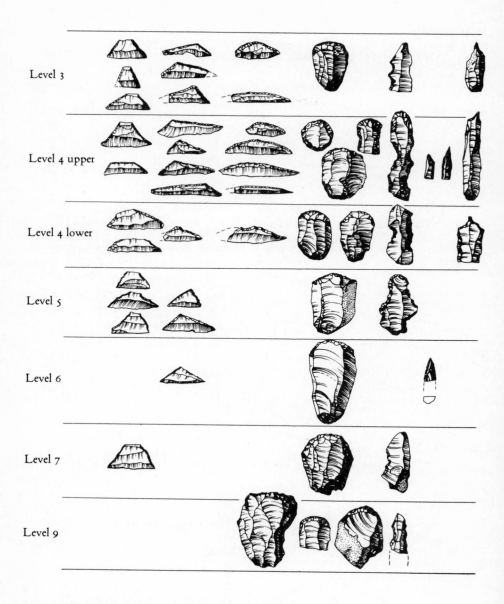

Level 3

Level 4 upper

Level 4 lower

Level 5

Level 6

Level 7

Level 9

Fig. 4 Chipped stone implements from the Dam-Dam-Chashma 2 cave. 1 : 2

Dam-Dam-Chashma 2 cave are clearly triangular and trapezoid in outline. Large scrapers, including those manufactured on flakes are also found here. Examples of a more evolved flint industry have been found in layers 5, and 4 'lower'. The number of geometric tools here is larger, and all are of a regular symmetrical form. By contrast, many trapezoid tools have concave edges. This is also true of the flint tools excavated in layers 3 and 2 containing pottery with incised and stamped decoration.

This stratigraphy of one of the Caspian caves is of great interest to archaeologists. Recent studies suggest that there may have been at least two variants of the Caspian Mesolithic. One of these variants is characterized by large asymmetrical trapezes with concave edges, long asymmetrical triangles and thin elongated, heavily retouched segments, as seen in the upper layer 4 at Dam-Dam-Chashma 2 cave, the bottom layer of Kailiu cave and Hodja-Su 1. These assemblages have strong connections with areas lying to the south-west, far beyond the limits of Turkmenia, that is, with the Zarzian tradition which was recently discovered in Iranian Kurdistan, and with the middle Mesolithic assemblage of the Mazanderan cave of Gari-Kamarband. The other variant is characterized by symmetrical or slightly asymmetrical trapezes with straight edges and right-angled triangles with sharply retouched corners, as seen in layers 7–5 in the Dam-Dam-Chashma 2 cave, and in the Late Mesolithic of Djebel which immediately precedes and then develops into the Neolithic with its crude hand-made pottery. Surprisingly, no geometric tools have been found in levels 8–7 of the Djebel cave, while in levels 6, 5–b, and 5–a, they re-emerge in the shape of small isosceles trapezes.[2]

It is not yet clear whether these two variants developed in the Caspian area with a parallel evolution, or whether one of them is the result of infiltrations by groups from the south. In Kailiu the material of the first variant lies right at the bottom of the cave, while in the Dam-Dam-Chashma 2 cave it intrudes in the evolution of the local tradition.

Unfortunately the lack of organic remains in the caves of the eastern Caspian area makes it difficult to determine their age by radiocarbon analysis. Judging by some analogies with the sites of Mazanderan (Hotu and Gari-Kamarband) the Mesolithic period of the eastern Caspian area could tentatively be dated to the tenth-sixth millennia BC and synchronized in its late stages with the Djeitun culture (sedentary agricultural settlements.)[3]

The main activities of the Mesolithic tribes of the eastern Caspian region were hunting and fishing. The osteological material shows that the principal game was onager and gazelle, with goat and sheep of secon׳dary importance. A similar situation is apparent on the southern coast of the Caspian Sea, where the inhabitants of levels 11–17 of the Gari׳Kamarband cave have been designated 'gazelle hunters'. Their other game included water fowl, fox and wild cat.

The Caspian Sea and the Uzboi, which in those days was a deep river, provided fish for the local Mesolithic population. The Kailiu cave contains large amounts of fish scales and fish bones, particularly those of sturgeon. Bones of carp and sturgeon come from the Djebel cave situated near the Uzboi which is now a dry river bed. However, the material excavated from the Gari׳Kamarband cave has led re׳searchers to believe that its inhabitants kept domesticated goats as far back as the seventh millennium BC. Level 4 of the Dam׳Dam׳Chashma 2 cave contained the skeletal remains of what was undoubtedly a domesticated goat, indicating that the first attempts at domestication were made earlier than the seventh millenium BC.[4] At present there is sufficient evidence to indicate that the beginnings of cattle breeding also date back to the Mesolithic period. In the mixed hunting/fishing/stock׳breeding economy of the Mesolithic tribes of the Caspian area, stock׳breeding was potentially the most promising for the growth of the economy, but the desert conditions of this region (particularly in the area east of the Caspian Sea) impeded the transition to a food׳production economy and thus encouraged the retention of archaic elements in the local culture. This also explains why agriculture did not develop beyond its incipient stage for such a long time. It is interesting to note in this respect the complete absence of sickle blades in the area east of the Caspian Sea, while in the area to the south only a few have been found. Unfortunately no Mesolithic material has been collected so far in the areas more favourable for food׳gathering and agriculture, especially in the Turkmeno׳Khorasan mountains.

THE WESTERN TADJIKISTAN GROUP

East of the Caspian, late Mesolithic implements found in the Kara Kum testify to the fact that this territory was once exploited by ancient hunters. A whole series of sites of this type was excavated in western Tadjikistan, where they comprise the second variant, or the second culture, of the Western Central Asian Mesolithic. These sites are located along the tributaries of the Amu Darya or near sources of fresh spring water. As a rule, a cultural layer has not been preserved and they are most likely the remains of temporary camp-sites. One of the earliest in this group is the site at Kui Bulien, where blades with blunted edges, points, and a number of geometric implements including a triangle have been found. The symmetrical trapezes and a small lunate from the site at Chil Chor Chashma may date to the Late Mesolithic period. No direct connection has so far been established between these finds and the material from the lower layer at Tutkaul (layer 3). This early assemblage includes small, almost rectangular trapezes, flake scrapers and large pointed scrapers. [5]

THE FERGANA VALLEY GROUP

Finally, the third group (or the third culture) of Mesolithic sites includes the open sites and caves of the Fergana Valley.[6] The flint implements, especially those from Late Mesolithic sites, are markedly microlithic, the principal blanks comprising micro-blades and tiny flakes. The only geometric tools are lunates. Most of the earlier material consists of large artifacts as seen at the Obi-Shir and Tash-Kumir caves. The objects found in the Fergana Valley are very much smaller in size than those recovered from caves near the Caspian Sea and in Western Tadjikistan.

It is interesting to note that a Mesolithic assemblage dating to the eighth millennium BC, with a wide use of micro-blades, was recently discovered in northern Afghanistan.[7]

THE EASTERN PAMIRS

The Mesolithic culture of the Eastern Pamirs is in many ways in a class by itself. Mesolithic implements have been recovered in about twenty places, including two large open sites—Karatumshuk and Oshkhona. These represent the traces of seasonal camp-sites of roving hunters who were attracted here by the abundance of game in the alpine meadows. The Oshkhona camp-site, where hearths have been discovered, lies by a stream which flows from a glacier, now 12 km. away. It is most likely that this was their 'summer retreat'. In winter the hunters descended to an area with a warmer climate. Bones of birds, rodents, mountain sheep

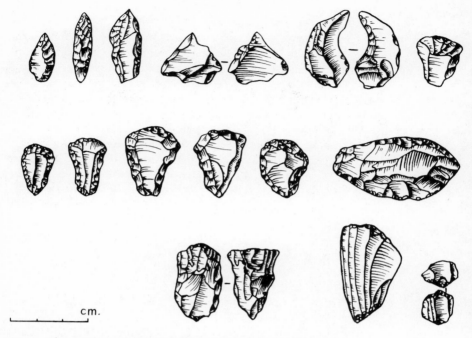

cm.

Fig. 5   Flint implements from the Mesolithic period of the Eastern Pamirs. 2 : 3

and goats found here give a good idea about the hunting activities of the Mesolithic inhabitants. The flint industry of the Eastern Pamirs is very unusual: crudely-made tools such as discoid cores, heavy scrapers, which look very much like Upper Palaeolithic artifacts from Siberia, and a large number of pebble-tools, including choppers retain superficially archaic forms. On the other hand the excavations at Oshkhona yielded numerous blade implements, such as thick blade scrapers, and backed blades. There were even arrow-heads with careless bifacial retouch. Radiocarbon analysis dated the Oshkhona material to 7580 ± 130 BC, which shows that its age is about the same as that of the Mesolithic material recovered near the Caspian Sea. These assemblages of the Eastern Pamirs are distinctly related to the Late Palaeolithic assemblages of the Siberian-Mongolian tradition.

Fig. 5

31

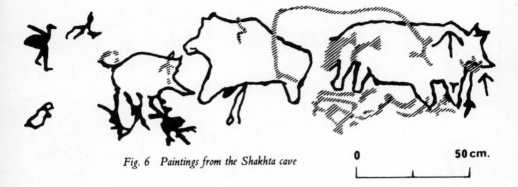

Fig. 6   Paintings from the Shakhta cave

0   50 cm.

Fig. 6

In the light of these connections the discovery in the Shakhta cave in the Eastern Pamirs of a painting executed in ochre mixed with animal fat is of great scientific interest. The painting is a typical hunting scene: the outlines of boars and a large animal, possibly a yak, being showered with flying arrows. Scenes of bulls and goats being hunted have also been painted on the walls of the Zaraut Kamar rock-shelter in southern Plate 2 Uzbekistan. The hunters here are portrayed in bell-shaped skirts, and the important fact is that the men in these paintings are assisted by dogs. Unlike the paintings in the Shakhta cave, the figures in the Zaraut Kamar cave are painted in silhouette, and not in outline. Both works are imbued with vital realism that goes back to the traditions of Upper Paleolithic art. The nature of the cultural layer in the Shakhta cave would suggest that these frescoes date to the Mesolithic or Early Neolithic period.

Thus the Mesolithic period in Western Central Asia saw the perfection of microlithic techniques and the initial stages of stock breeding;[8] but these were only the precursors of the important changes that were to take place in the future.

CHAPTER IV

The Djeitun Culture : Incipient Civilization

In the Neolithic period, there developed a qualitatively new economy, the production economy, a transformation which Gordon Childe called, with good reasons, 'the Neolithic revolution'. This transition began with the domestication of animals and plants and ended at a time when the new sources accounted for more than 50% of all the foodstuffs consumed. Such archaic branches of the economy as hunting, fishing and food gathering retained high economic potential and could still be used if the conditions so required, although the essence of the economic transformation remained unchanged.

The Neolithic revolution did not develop everywhere in the same manner; in the Near East, for example, two variants have been observed —one predominantly agricultural and the other predominantly pastoral. Judging by the available evidence, these two variants were also represented in the area of Western Central Asia. While in northern and eastern Turkmenia stock-breeding developed very early, although slowly, as a new mode of procuring food, in southern Turkmenia it was developed in association with the cultivation of plants, the farmers leading a more settled way of life.

This process is best illustrated by the Djeitun culture. It is characterized by a microlithic flint industry and geometric tools, one-roomed houses, built of cylindrical clay bricks, and flat-bottomed pots made of chaff-tempered ware, decorated with simple painted patterns. At present we can speak of three periods within the Djeitun culture.[1] The first period includes the site of Djeitun, the lower layers of Chopan-depe, and the lower layer of Togolok-depe. The middle period is represented in the upper layers of Chopan-depe, Togolok-depe, Bami, Novaya Nisa, Pessedjik-depe and the lower layers of Mondjukli-depe and Chagilli-depe. The late period of the Djeitun culture is best illustrated by the material from the upper layers of Chagilli-depe. The Djeitun culture is represented at this site in habitation levels 15–18, which correspond to a period of about one thousand years.[2] The Late Djeitun levels at Chagilli-depe have been dated by the C-14 method to 5050 ± 110 BC.

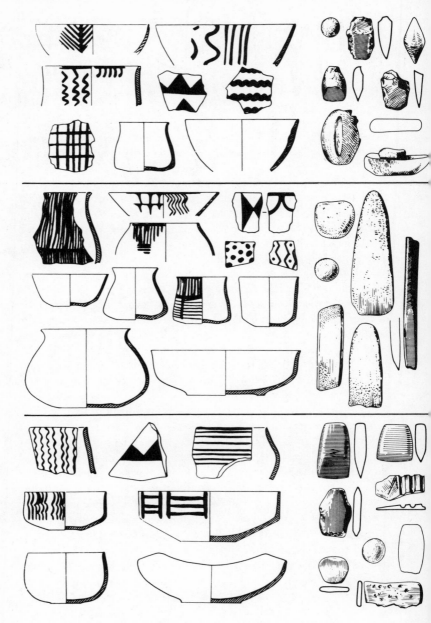

Fig. 7   *The Djeitun culture : artifacts of the early, middle and late phases*

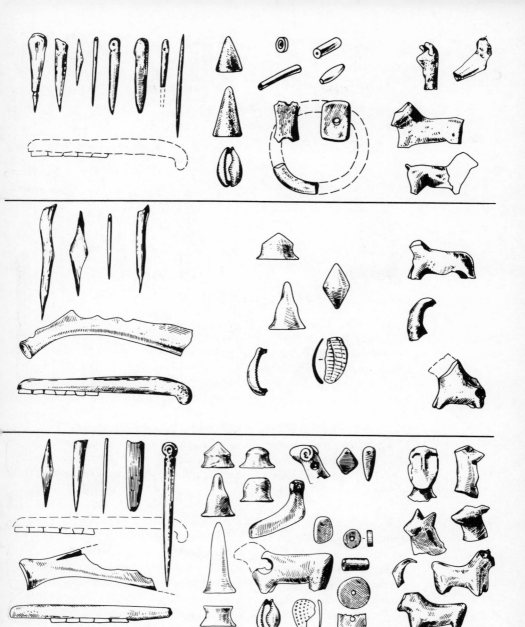

35

Fig. 8 Djeitun culture flints of the early, middle and late phases

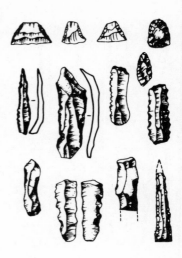

Figs. 7, 8

The material of the early phase of the Djeitun culture has analogies in the upper layers of Jarmo and Tepe Guran,[3] while the material of the middle and, to a certain extent, the late period is similar to that of the Sialk-I assemblage. This allows us to date the Djeitun culture to the sixth millennium BC. New progressive features are evident in literally all aspects of the economy and activities of these ancient inhabitants of southern Turkmenistan. The settled way of life which came with the establishment of the new economy led to the emergence of permanent settlements. From now on it was not the natural protection of caves or light shacks on open sites, but sturdy clay-brick houses that gave shelter to man.

Plate 3

The village of Djeitun is characteristic of the early period. The settlement itself once stood at the top of a sandy hill on the southern edge of the Kara Kum Desert. Houses here were constructed of clay bricks, heavily tempered with chaff straw, some 60–70 cm. long and with an oval section of 10–25 cm. in diameter. The walls inside were daubed with a clay-and-water solution and were sometimes painted red or black. The floor in such houses was, as a rule, covered with lime plaster 1.0–1.5 cm. thick and painted the same colour as the walls. Sometimes the floor was nothing but a hard beaten surface with ashes spread on top.

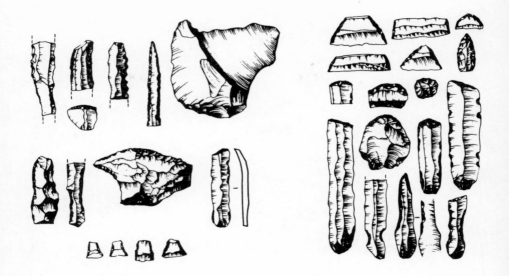

All the houses at Djeitun were built to the same plan with standard proportions and dimensions; they were rectangular, or almost square in plan. Since evidence of wooden doors has so far not been found, it is quite possible that the narrow door-way was merely covered with mats or curtained with animal skins. Inside the house, on the right of the door-way, was a large rectangular hearth. Some of the hearths had narrow platforms in front with raised edges onto which the burnt wood and ashes were raked. The part of the house between the hearth and the doorway was often partitioned off by a low wall and may possibly have been used for storage. On the wall opposite the hearth was a rectangular projection low down just above the floor inside which was a small niche; in many houses, these projections and the floors were painted red or black. In the corner of one of the houses a storage pit had been dug into the floor; its walls were lined with well-levigated fired clay. This was the standard plan for all Djeitun houses. The only marked variation was in the position of the hearth: sometimes it stood by the northern wall and sometimes by the eastern. In the period of the second building level, Djeitun consisted of thirty such houses, whose area varied from 13 sq. m. to 39 sq. m. with an average of 20–30 sq. m., large enough to house one nuclear family.

Plate 6
Fig. 9

37

Each house had a courtyard with out-houses in it; these courtyards varied in size, and indeed very often two houses shared a single one between them. In various parts of the village, structures were excavated which most likely represent the foundations of platforms for grain storage. They consist of two rather squat parallel walls, high enough from the ground to ensure aeration of the grain. On the edge of the village structures were built with walls which were thicker than elsewhere, but no one great wall encircled the settlement.

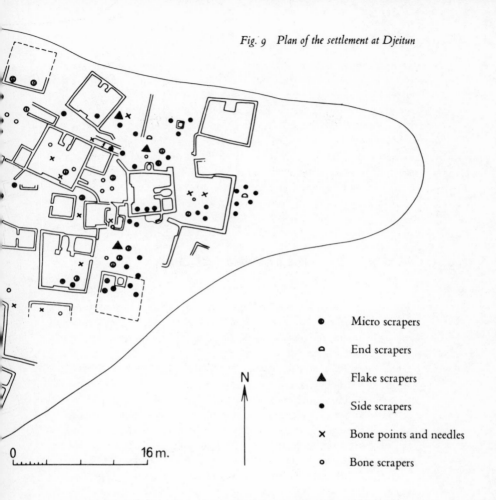

Fig. 9 Plan of the settlement at Djeitun

●	Micro scrapers
◠	End scrapers
▲	Flake scrapers
●	Side scrapers
✕	Bone points and needles
○	Bone scrapers

N

0   16 m.

These one-roomed houses were a characteristic feature of the Djeitun culture throughout the entire period of its existence. Similar houses representing the middle Djeitun period have been excavated in the villages of Chopan-depe, Togolok-depe and Pessedjik-depe. However, the floors of these houses were often covered not with lime plaster, but with a thin clay layer, on top of which lay woven reed-mats. Of special interest is the discovery, in Pessedjik-depe, of a house with a white lime-plastered floor about 64 sq. m. in area. Its large dimensions

39

and the small number of domestic artifacts it contained suggest that it was a kind of club-house or communal meeting place, possibly a cult centre. The interior arrangement of this house does not differ from that of ordinary dwellings. In the early stage of the Djeitun culture, judging from the excavations at Djeitun itself, such club-houses did not yet exist. We should note here that in the settlement of Bami, which is situated closer to the mountains than any other Djeitun site, walls constructed of stone have been found.

This basic house-building tradition continued in the late period of the Djeitun culture. Alongside clay blocks used for building, flat bricks came into use. One-roomed houses with floors, which were sometimes painted red or black, have been discovered in two upper building levels of Chagilli-depe, a small settlement consisting of 12–14 houses. The stone door-sockets found at this site indicate the use of hinged doors.

POTTERY AND ARTIFACTS

The settled way of life and the intensive exploitation of plant foods by the Djeitun people was accompanied by the appearance of pottery. This was chaff tempered rouletted ware made by hand, and given a carefully polished surface. In the early period about 12% of the pottery was decorated by red painted patterns on a yellowish background. Most of the vessels thus decorated were cylindro-conical bowls. The painted patterns were simple, consisting mainly of parallel rows of wavy lines and vertical bracket-like lines, and triangular patterns were fairly rare. The range of forms of the early Djeitun pottery is rather primitive and the whole complex has an archaic appearance. The quadrangular bowls possibly imitate pre-ceramic basket containers.

In the middle period of the Djeitun culture the pottery forms become more varied. The painted pottery of this period excavated at Chopan-depe forms only about 3% of the total pottery. The percentage is slightly higher in the corresponding layers of Togolok-depe. Here the wavy lines and bracket-like patterns give way to finely reticulated designs and dotted patterns. Triangles are more common than in the earlier stages. The pottery decoration becomes more dissected and diminutive in the third period when designs were often painted also on the inner surface of the pots. The decoration is in the form of undulating horizontal lines, vertical zigzags, and tree-like patterns.

The Djeitun production tools combine traditional, archaic and new progressive elements. The wear-traces of these tools have been studied, greatly increasing our knowledge of the economic organization of this Neolithic society. One of the basic features of the Djeitun culture was the markedly microlithic nature of its flint blade industry, which suggests some sort of genetic connection with the Mesolithic of the Caspian area; at the same time, it is well in advance of all the previous Mesolithic traditions. The early period is noted for the high frequency of geometric microliths which account for 5.4% of all the tools. These are mainly regular trapezes, although lunates and triangles also occur. In the middle period geometric microliths decrease. Mesolithic traditions are very pronounced in such commonly used tools as notched shavers and gravers. But the most important of these tools fashioned in the traditional Mesolithic techniques are sickles, which were of the greatest importance for the Djeitun agriculturists. It is no accident that sickle blades form 37% of the total number of tools found at Djeitun, and 31% at Chagilli-depe. These blades were inserted into straight bone handles, and for this reason preference was given to thin blades with sharp unretouched edges. Some of these blades are of trapezoid shape. In the middle period of the Djeitun culture the sickle blades were larger and heavier; those with denticulated cutting edges were at first rather rare, but their number markedly increased in later periods.

A large number of flint and bone tools were used for processing skins. Thus tools made of animals' shoulder blades were used for cleaning in the initial stage of dressing skins, in which unretouched blade tools, referred to by G. F. Korobkova as 'side scrapers', were also used. In the subsequent stages of processing skins a wide variety of microlithic scrapers was employed, including pointed ones. The latter were used for removing pockets of fat and dead tissue from the cleaned surface. In the late period of the Djeitun culture the number of scraping tools decreased, which is attributed to the development of weaving techniques. Bones were used mostly in the manufacture of awls and needles.

Also found, though far less frequently, are polished stone tools, among them smooth flat discs of irregular shape, sandstone pestles and mortars for grinding red ochre, and querns; likewise axe-adzes, mostly of small size, and—at Chopan-depe—a stone chisel believed to have been used for wood-trimming.

Plate 4

41

Numerous artifacts found on sites of the Djeitun culture which are not directly connected with production indicate the relative prosperity of the Djeitun people and also the fact that they had a fair amount of leisure time. These include stone and baked clay objects in the shape of complete cones, truncated cones, etc. Though views differ as to their purpose, these objects show traces of wear which suggest that they were used as counters in some game.[4] There is also a variety of pendants and beads, the latter made of bone, sea shells, stone (including turquoise) and even of clay, and pendants in the form of stone figurines of animals.

The clay figurines of humans and animals were most likely used as fetishes and amulets; these include human heads modelled in a flat, stylized manner. Some of the animal figurines obviously represent goats, and others bovids. Many figurines of unbaked clay have holes made with sharp sticks which are probably the traces of some magical ritual; indeed at Chagilli-depe a figurine has been found with a sharp needle still sticking into it.

ECONOMY

All the new features of the Djeitun culture—a firmly settled population, clay brick architecture, and a better standard of living—are expressions of the social transformation brought about by the Neolithic revolution, which established an economic system based on agriculture and stock-breeding, the two mainstays of the food-production economy. In Djeitun alone 1,057 flint sickle blades have been found. Even on a conservative estimate of 1–3 blades per sickle, this would place the number of reaping tools at about 500–600, implying that each of the thirty families living in Djeitun replaced about twenty reaping knives over the period spanned by the second occupation level. Impressions of stalks and grains, as well as the grains of cultivated plants themselves, have been discovered in settlements of the Djeitun culture. At Chagilli-depe the grains of *Hordeum disticum* (two row barley), *Triticum vulgare* and *Triticum compactum* (wheat) have been identified.

The Djeitun sites themselves are located on the narrow submontane plateau hemmed in between the spurs of the Kopet Dag and the sand-dunes of the Kara Kum Desert, with a dry climate (the annual rainfall at present does not exceed 285 mm.) It is reasonable to suppose that the population of the Djeitun sites used some primitive form of irrigation such as spring and summer flooding. Djeitun itself lies on the delta of a large mountain stream.

It is not yet clear how the fields were worked. None of the Djeitun sites have produced stone mattocks. It would seem that the principal agricultural tools at that time were made of wood and probably had not developed far beyond the digging-stick. It was only in the later stages of the Djeitun culture that there is evidence that ring-weights were attached to the sticks to increase their efficiency.

The following figures show the tremendous economic effect of agriculture. The population of Djeitun, where the houses of 30 nuclear families have been excavated, consisted of about 150–180 people. Estimated at 1 kg. of grain per person a day (such averages are indicated in Sumerian written records), the annual grain demand for the whole community thus comprises 44 tons which, at a low crop ratio of 15, would require a sowing area of $87\frac{1}{2}$ acres. In present-day northern Iraq, with its backward fragmented cultivation system, the working of 15 acres would require 250 man-days of labour. Taking this norm as a basis, 1,000 man-days of labour would be sufficient to work $37\frac{1}{2}$ acres. If the lower efficiency of agricultural implements is taken into account, this figure could be raised to 3,000 man-days. And even then, two adults from each family in Neolithic Djeitun would take about two months to cope with the job. It has been proved by experiment that with a stone-edged sickle an unskilled person can collect 1.5 kg. of grain an hour. Thus, working 10 hours a day, Neolithic farmers could have collected 50 tons of grain for 1,600 man-hours of labour. In other words, three workers from each Djeitun family could have completed the reaping in 17–18 days. Approximate as these estimates are (the time necessary for the manufacture of tools, processing of grain, preparation of food, etc. has not been calculated), they give a fairly good picture of the colossal economic effect of agriculture.

However, agriculture was not the only economic innovation of the Djeitun culture; it developed alongside stock-breeding, which as we noted before, was the second mainstay of the production economy. Recent studies indicate that even in the early period of the Djeitun culture domesticated goats and sheep supplied most of the meat in the diet. The shape of the horns of the goats proves that these animals were domesticated and not wild; in the latest period of the Djeitun culture, moreover, the abundant osteological evidence from the upper layers of Chagilli-depe, points to cattle also having been domesticated. The character of the Neolithic pastoralism of southern Turkmenia is not yet clear. In none of the settlements excavated so far is there any evidence of corrals or stables, although some of the ancillary structures that clustered round the houses may well have been used for this purpose. The most likely method of animal husbandry in those days was pasturing. Dogs could have been used to guard the cattle, canine bones having been found among the Djeitun osteological material.

In the early period, at least, of the Djeitun culture, a major part was played in the economy by hunting for gazelle, onager, wild pig and sheep, as well as fur-bearing animals such as fox (9 individuals), cat (2 individuals) and wolf (3 individuals). Gazelle *(gazella subgutturosa)*, which was a favourite quarry of the Djeitun hunters, was rounded up in large numbers. It is interesting to note that no arrow-heads or spear-heads have been found among the flint implements of Djeitun. It is possible that missile weapons were constructed by inserting heads of geometric microliths into wooden shafts. The sling was also widely used, besides which sling-stones may have been projected by a special bow, a modern version of which is still used in sharp-shooting competitions. In the later periods of the Djeitun culture the importance of hunting decreased considerably. The marked predominance of the bones of domesticated animals in the Chagilli-depe material gives a picture very close to that of the Chalcolithic settlements.

The production and procurement of food formed the basis of the Djeitun economy, and led to the development of a whole series of subsidiary domestic activities. The excavations at the Djeitun site provide a very fine picture of such activities. They were all of an essentially decentralized character. Each family was engaged separately in the manufacture of tools, in the processing of skins, in wood-working and preparing food. This can be seen by the complete absence of large vessels for use by the whole community. Most of the tools have been found in the courtyards, showing that this was the main working area. It should be remembered that specialist craftsmen had not yet separated from the community to such an extent that it is visible in the archaeological evidence. The Djeitun community was an amalgamation of nuclear families, each of which produced domestic tools and other household

Plate 7

requisites. Unlike Anatolia, with its large centres such as Çatal Hüyük, neolithic Turkmenia was a country of small and rather poor villages.

It has now been established beyond any doubt that the people who adopted the Djeitun culture maintained connections with the early agriculturists of the Near East. This is reflected above all in specific features of Djeitun architecture such as the lime coating of the floor, as well as in the painting of the floor and walls. Such painting characterized the architecture of Pre-pottery Jericho in the eighth–seventh millennia BC and originated, not among the inhabitants of caves and rock-shelters of that area, but in open villages similar to Natufian Eynan in Palestine. Stone and clay gaming counters, small stone axes, baked clay figurines, the wide use of ochre and a whole set of associated tools were also features common in many early farming communities of the Near East.

At the same time, inside this vast zone two main cultural areas may be distinguished: the Syro-Palestinian–Asia Minor group, and the Iraqo-Iranian group. Within each of these areas there were a number of cultures and culture complexes. In the Iraqo-Iranian zone the best documented is the Zagros Mountain region—Jarmo, Sarab and Tepe Guran; this offers the clearest analogies to the Djeitun culture, especially in flint implements and pottery, though there are also important differences which distinguish the two cultures. For example, the sickle found in Jarmo is curved, while the reaping knife from Djeitun is straight; the hearths are of a different design, and no stone bracelets have been found among the Djeitun artifacts.

In this respect it is worth noting some analogies between the late Djeitun sites and the material of Sialk I in Central Iran. These parallels between the two include straight reaping knives, stone and baked clay counters and certain elements of pottery decoration. The impression is that the Sialk I complex had, as its basis, local Neolithic traditions of the Djeitun type, along with western influence of the late Jarmo and Hassuna cultures. It is very significant, therefore, that the pottery excavated from the lower occupation levels of Yarim-tepe in northern Iran is in many ways similar to that of Djeitun. It is quite possible that northern Iran and southern Turkmenia shared a common Djeitun culture which, alongside the Zagros culture, formed the Iraqo-Iranian area of early farming cultures.

Unfortunately there is so far no archaeological evidence of cultural connections prior to the early phase of the Djeitun culture. Broadly speaking, we may say that the Djeitun culture had the Mesolithic horizon of both southern Central Asia and northern Iran as its basis. This is borne out by a number of analogies between Djeitun and the Caspian Mesolithic, and it would seem from a comparison of the flint industries of Djeitun and those of the Djebel cave, as well as the close resemblance of the geometric tools, gravers, scrapers, awls and drills, that these two groups developed along similar lines. Cones of unbaked clay, analogous with the terracotta counters from Djeitun, have been found in the cave of Gari-Kamarband in northern Iran. Excavations in this cave also produced a stone pendant resembling a sitting human figure very similar to its Djeitun equivalents. It is quite possible that these Mesolithic hunters and food-gatherers of the Turkmeno-Khorasan Mountains, having a culture very close to that of the Caspian Mesolithic, were the ancestors of the bearers of the Djeitun culture, which was at the same time greatly influenced by the highly developed centres of the Near East. The Djeitun culture was in fact one manifestation of the complicated process of transition to a production economy which in the eighth–sixth millennia BC embraced vast areas of the Near East. It is not surprising that it was in the south that this transition precipitated a rapid cultural florescence in the fifth–fourth millennia BC.

CHAPTER V

Early Chalcolithic Cultures in Turkmenia

In Western Central Asia, as in many other areas, the Chalcolithic is linked with early agricultural cultures. It was in this period that the beneficial effects of the transition to a food-production economy, which had been only faintly suggested in the archaic Djeitun culture, fully manifested themselves.

The excavations undertaken by the Russian general Komarov and, later, by the American expedition under the direction of Pumpelly at the Anau mounds supplied archaeological information about the Chalco-lithic material of southern Turkmenia. As a result, the first chronological classification of the local mixed-farming cultures (Anau I-IV) was established.

This stratigraphical sequence was based mainly on successive changes in the ceramic styles. Schmidt, on the basis of the pottery confined in it, divided the lowest cultural layer of the northern mound at Anau (Anau I) into two sub-periods, the oldest of which was designated Anau I-A. Subsequent research showed that this subdivision of the Anau I period was correct. The pottery of Anau I-A is very different from the pottery of the Djeitun Neolithic, which was made of chaff-tempered fabric while the pottery of Anau I-A is noted for its ample sand admixture, well-levigated clay, and skilled firing. The thin-walled, gracefully-shaped vessels, mainly drinking bowls, with painted geo-metric decoration featuring large figures filled with cross-hatching, compare favourably with the Djeitun pottery. A characteristic feature of the Anau I-A pottery vessels is their concave bases.

Fig. 10

Until the end of the Second World War the Anau I-A complex was associated only with material excavated from the northern mound of Anau. But extensive post-war research has yielded many more sites of this type over a wide area. For example, the lower occupation levels of the ancient agricultural settlement of Govich-depe, west of Anau, contained pottery typical of Anau I-A. More information was recently obtained from sites such as Koushut, Mondjukli, and Chakmakli.

47

Fig. 10   Painted pottery of Anau I-A type

Although the excavations at Koushut, east of Anau, mainly took the form of probes, the trial trench cut through the middle of the mound revealed several cultural layers with a total thickness of 3.5 m. The pottery excavated here had as decoration geometric patterns filled with cross-hatching. The finds included spindle-whorls and occasional

copper objects including a heavy awl. On the whole the forms and painted decoration of the Koushut pottery can hardly be matched with those of Anau I-A; their analogies may be found primarily at Chak-makli and Mondjukli in south-eastern Turkmenia.

Chakmakli (Mound of Flints), is situated near the village of Chaacha and comprises a shallow mound, measuring 80 × 60 m. and a little over

1.5 m. high. From an examination of the underlying sedimentary rock, it is clear that Chakmakli-depe was situated in the flood plain of a large delta channel, and at the outset must have frequently suffered from seasonal inundations. A trial trench cut through the centre of the settlement to a depth of 2.85 m., revealed a total of five building levels; in the second, third and fourth levels, walls constructed of rectangular

sun-baked bricks measuring 50 × 20 × 10 cm. were discovered. The walls and floors were covered with clay plaster. A layer of alluvial sand 50 cm. thick was found between the fourth and fifth building levels.

Although the lowest or fifth level contained charcoal and flint chips, as well as a few fragments of copper (discovered in 1968), it is remarkable

that no pottery was found; this absence of pottery makes the whole picture very confusing. On the other hand, the pottery of the fourth level, immediately above, is shapely, well fired and decorated with relatively intricate painted patterns. The excavation of the uppermost building level has yielded a larger number of artifacts. Although the dwellings in this first level were completely destroyed, some large frag-ments of floor have survived with traces of red paint.

In the second building level, which was excavated over a large area, houses constructed of bricks were preserved up to a height of 0.5 m. Here more than 30 living and working areas were cleared. They were divided by a narrow central lane into two separate agglomerated com-plexes. In general there were two types of room: small ones with a hearth in the corner (kitchens) and larger elongated ones, with numerous projections on the inside walls (living rooms). On the whole Chak-makli-depe was well-planned, with all its houses and even separate

Fig. 11   Painted pottery of Chakmakli-depe type

rooms connected and complementing one another. In each of these complexes one of the rooms which was excavated had the walls and floors painted red. These rooms may have had a ritualistic significance.

All the pottery, both from the trial trench and from the building level described above, belongs to one ceramic complex. The fabric was tempered with sand and well-fired. The vessel most frequently encountered was the thin-walled red- or yellow-slipped hemispherical bowl, sometimes burnished, with flat or concave base. The most common decoration consisted of hatched triangles and a combined pattern of slanting parallel lines and triangles executed in black paint. Burins, drills, scrapers and blade inserts for sickles and reaping knives were made of white transluscent flint. In addition stone querns, and mortars and

Fig. 11

Plate 5

pounders were relatively numerous. New types of tools included chisels, which were most likely used for woodwork, and two hoes made of a black stone. The few heavy copper articles were used as tools and not as ornaments. Fired clay spindle-whorls occurred fairly frequently.

The third site with a similar assemblage is Mondjukli-depe, situated near the village of Chaacha, although the material from this interesting site has not yet been fully published. A trial trench was cut through the mound to bedrock. Judging by the material obtained from this trench the lower levels of Mondjukli-depe belong to the Neolithic Djeitun culture. A large area of the upper building level, which contained material typical of Chakmakli-depe was excavated. Besides similar pottery, a number of clay spindle-whorls and sporadic copper tools were found here. The excavated upper building level consists of two rows of living and working rooms divided by a central lane into roughly two large agglomerated complexes. At Mondjukli-depe the archaic neolithic influences of Djeitun are more pronounced than at Chakmakli, as seen in the general planning of the settlement, which consisted mainly of one-roomed houses.

CHRONOLOGY AND RELATIONSHIPS

It is quite clear that the early Chalcolithic complex of the Chakmakli type preceded the Anau complex, and held a transitional position in the development of the local mixed farming culture. Until recently, all this pre-Anau material, irrespective of its geographical position, was classed as the Anau I-A complex; such a rough division is no longer satis-factory and the material requires a more detailed classification.

On the basis of the available evidence it has been suggested that only the lower layer of the north mound at Anau and the settlement at Govich-depe belong to the Anau I-A culture, since both contain pottery painted with rhomboids, flanked by two triangles. This motif is entirely un-known in south-eastern Turkmenia. J. McCowan, the first to study the origin of the Anau I-A complex, established analogies with the painted ware of Sialk II, and suggested that the Anau I-A material should be related to the Chashma Ali culture. Recent excavations at the Teheran Oasis (Ismailabad, Kara-depe) show that it is to the material of this oasis that the Anau I-A complex comes closest, however, and not to that of Sialk.

The question of the pre-Anau complex of south-eastern Turkmenia is rather different. The decoration of the painted pottery from Koushut, Chakmakli and the upper layers of Mondjukli is similar in certain respects to the decoration of the 'standard' ware of Hassuna IV-V type. In addition, hoes of Hassuna type have been found at Chakmakli. This may denote the north-easternmost extension of Hassuna-Sialk influence. As has been pointed out in the literature, the pottery of Hassana IV-V type has its equivalents in the pottery of Sialk I3, which may reflect Hassuna influence extending from Mesopotamia across the Zagros mountains, as far as the central regions of Iran. It is quite possible that, early in the fifth millennium BC there were considerable population movements in what is now Iran, which may have impinged on the fertile valleys of south-eastern Turkmenia. It is still hard to say when and why these migrations occurred. The very fact that in Mondjukli-depe the pre-Anau layers overlap the middle Djeitun layers, shows that this process took place as early as the Neolithic period. Moreover, it has been suggested that, for a certain time, the newcomers co-existed with the local tribes of the Djeitun culture, but further support is needed for this hypothesis.

One should not, however, oversimplify the process which established the early Chalcolithic communities in southern Turkmenia. This complicated process was, on the one hand, determined by the progressive economic development of the entire preceding Neolithic period, and, on the other, by the innovations which were brought by the newcomers themselves. Thus, the earliest metal-smelting techniques must have been imported, as there are no known copper deposits in the northern Kopet Dag, whereas the material from Sialk I has led us to believe that one of the oldest centres of metal-smelting was in Iran. It is also very significant that all the known copper artifacts of the pre-Anau period were production tools (awls, a piercer, a fragment of a double-bladed knife), and not ornaments. It has been assumed that in this period ore was imported from Iran to southern Turkmenia where it was processed. Although primitive weaving originated as early as the Late Djeitun period (Chagilli), there is evidence that the fired clay spindle-whorls were associated with these newcomers.

The above account should not be allowed to obscure the fact that in general the newcomers were soon absorbed into the local population

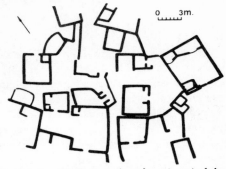

*Figs 12, 13   Namazga I-type assem-
blage, from Dashlidji-depe. Right, settlement type; far right, pottery, figurines,
and artifacts of stone, copper, bone and clay*

and adopted many of its cultural traits. We have only to bear in mind the
standard shape of bricks, the design of the hearths, and the decoration of
the interior of houses, *i.e.* the typically Djeitun building traditions which
were widely used in the pre-Anau villages of Mondjukli-depe and
Chakmakli-depe. In other words, among the south Turkmenian
tribes there was a general evolution in both their economy and culture
throughout the fifth millennium BC. The accumulation of practical
knowledge, improvement of agricultural techniques, the resulting
higher crop yields and important developments in cattle breeding all
tended to cause a sharp increase in the chalcolithic population.

GROWTH AND EXPANSION: ANAU I—NAMAZGA I

Thus, during the subsequent Anau I–Namazga I culture, the scattered
villages of the preceding period were gradually replaced by a whole chain

Fig. 14   of early agricultural settlements that stretched along the foothills of the
Kopet Dag. At that time the submontane oases and other fertile areas
were put to good use. The greater number of settlements is not the only
indication of the advent of a new epoch, another being the qualitative
changes in their development. Alongside small villages of a few acres,
there were also large settlements, with an area of 35 acres or more (Kara-
depe, Namazga-depe).

The exploitation of new oases indicates the growth of an extensive
food-production economy. Local agriculturalists cultivated *Triticum
vulgare* (wheat) and *Hordeum disticum* (two-row barley). The erratic
submontane rivers and streams, as well as the wide channels in deltas
created favourable conditions for irrigation farming. The fields were
tilled with digging-sticks weighted by stone rings, and the grain was
harvested by means of sickles fitted with flint or, possibly, copper
blades.

52

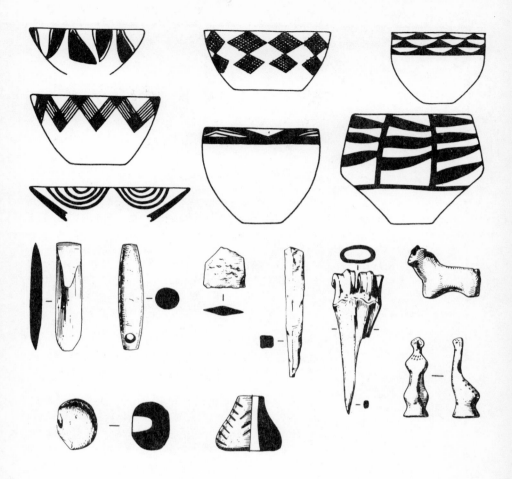

Stock-breeding was very important in the economy, whereas hunting activities played only a subsidiary role. For example, the bones of domestic animals recovered from Dashlidji-depe formed 80% of the total osteological material.

Flint tools were gradually replaced by those of copper. Weaving developed still further, as indicated by the large number of baked clay spindle-whorls which, together with pottery make up the bulk of the material excavated at Dashlidji-depe.

Fig. 13

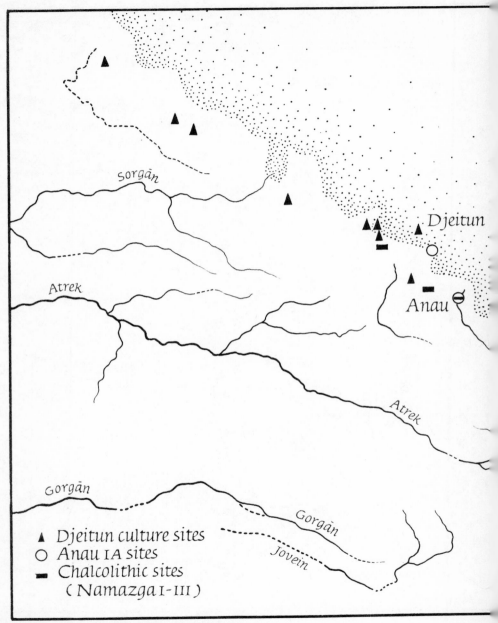

Fig. 14 *The early agricultural sites of Turkmenia*

0   100 Mls

0   150 Kms

Kara-depe

Geoksyur

Tedjen

Ulug-depe

Altin-depe

Kesnefrood

The buildings of the small villages show by their nature that their inhabitants may have lived as nuclear families who shared equal rights in the community. The grave goods, at any rate, give no ground to suppose that property inequality existed at that time. At the same time rapid economic progress and the associated improvement in the social life of the community stimulated the development of culture and the arts.[1] It is worth examining in detail the material dating back to the Anau I– Namazaga I period, in southern Turkmenia. Altogether, about twenty settlements are known from this period, which may be grouped into three geographical areas.

The first, or western, zone occupies the territory between Kizil Arvat and Anau. It includes the following settlements: Beurme, Karantki Tokai, Tilkin-depe, Dashli, Ovadan, Ekin-depe, Ak-depe, and Anau. Each village in this group generally occupies an area of about $2\frac{1}{2}$ acres and rises 2–3 m. above the surrounding area. Unfortunately the villages of the western zone have been studied very perfunctorily, using only material collected on the surface; very few have been investigated by trial excavations. This meagre evidence, however, is sufficient to indicate that the population of these villages pursued a mixed-farming economy, and that their houses were built of rectangular sun-baked bricks. Certain features of the pottery decoration (painted ribbon patterns, fuzzy lines, etc.) are characteristic of the sites of the western group.

The central zone occupies the area between Anau and Dushak. It includes large settlements such as Kara-depe and Namazga-depe and many smaller villages, such as Yassi-depe and Sermancha-depe. Material found on the surface indicates that there may also be layers dating to this period at Ulug-depe, near Dushak. All the sites are located in the most fertile and, once, well watered oases on the plateau north of the Kopet Dag mountains, in southern Turkmenia.

The third, eastern group includes the settlements situated in the lower courses of the Chaacha-Sai and Meana-Sai (Iilginli-depe, Altin-depe).

Unfortunately the Namazga I levels of sites in the foot-hills of the Kopet Dag have been examined only by trial trenches, so that the information about them is as yet very incomplete. The only exception is the excavation on the southern side of Kara-depe, in which was revealed a section of a large building inside which were dug large underground pits for storing food and chambers lined with potsherds, possibly for preserving products from damp.

The houses were generally built of standard rectangular sun-baked bricks tempered with chopped straw. The walls were covered with clay plaster, sometimes painted black. Stone sockets suggest that the doors were once made of wooden boards.

Alongside the living and store rooms, rooms believed to have been shrines have been excavated. The interior of one such room in the northern mound at Anau, is decorated with two rectangular panels of wall paintings. One of these bore red triangles, enclosed in black frames, the other red chequered squares.

More definite information of cult architecture has been found in the settlement of Yassi-depe. Here a shrine has been excavated in the centre of the village, consisting of two adjacent rooms connected by a passage. One of the rooms has a hearth, closely resembling those of the Djeitun culture, which may have served as a kind of altar. On the walls fragments of frescoes have been preserved.

In the second room, the wall opposite the entrance is covered with a polychrome painting several layers thick. On the earliest layer were painted vertical rows of rhomboids in different colours: first a row of black rhomboids, then a row of red rhomboids enclosed in black frames, and so on. On one of the later layers of the fresco were painted vertical rows of triangles in red, fringed with white alabaster incrustation. Along the other two walls in this room, at a short distance out from them, stand several wooden pillars. The wall painting and the colonnade must have given the whole place an awe-inspiring appearance. The above-mentioned polychrome paintings are the oldest frescoes ever found on the territory of the Soviet Union.

The pottery of this period was made of clay tempered with chaff. Although no kilns have been found, there is some evidence that the pottery was fired in primitive ovens, rather than in pits. The unpainted, coarse ware was used mostly for cooking. The large vessels were rounded in shape and made of clay mixed with heat-resistant materials.

Almost 30% of the fine ware is decorated with painted designs, of which the most typical comprise horizontal rows of triangles in black or dark-brown. In addition, there are bizarre patterns of zigzags, chequers, wavy lines and, more rarely, outlined portrayals of goats and plants.

A pottery fragment found at this site is decorated with the representation of an onager and a horse. Some vessels were painted inside and out.

On the whole, the shapes of vessels in this period were still clearly evolved from pottery of preceding periods. In this respect it is interesting to note vessels with concave bases which occasionally even flare out to form ring bases, a feature which was completely absent from the Djeitun pottery. On the other hand the basic painted patterns derived their inspiration from both the Djeitun and the Anau I-A pottery, while in general the features of the pottery of this period as a whole are common to all the zones of southern Turkmenia.

Plate 9
The few human figurines found here contrast with the schematic figurines of the Djeitun culture in their more realistic portrayal. One of the best examples is the female figurine from Kara-depe; unfortunately, the head was broken off in antiquity, but the body testifies to a good understanding of human anatomy. Its thin neck is encircled by a painted stripe like a ring which continues down the back in two bands. A second figurine with conical breasts and marked steatopygous features was found at this site. It is interesting to note that almost all the known anthropomorphic figurines are portrayed in a standing position. Later, however, until the end of the second millennium BC the seated position was more common.

Plate 8
The number of zoomorphic figurines (mostly sheep and cattle) is much greater. Made for the most part of unfired clay, they are usually modelled very schematically.

Tools include bone and copper piercers, sporadic flint blades, grind-stones, a large number of conical clay (less often stone) spindle-whorls, some of which are decorated. Ornaments include a few copper miniature pins with pyramidal knobs, as well as beads and pendants made of turquoise, carnelian and other semi-precious stones.

The dead were buried within the area of the settlement. Skeletons, both of children and of adults, were buried in a contracted position with their heads facing south; the funeral offerings are rather poor, mostly personal ornaments such as beads, copper tubes, and so on.

THE GEOKSYUR OASIS

As is clear from this account our knowledge of the economy, culture and history of the tribes which lived north of the Kopet Dag in the fourth millennium BC is very sketchy. The gaps may be filled to a certain extent by a study of the settlements of the Geoksyur Oasis in the ancient delta of the Tedjen River. The excavations carried out here over a wide area show that all the villages without exception were founded late in the Anau I–Namazga I period, whereas the villages in the foothills of the Kopet Dag mountains date to Neolithic and early Chalcolithic times.

In Turkmenia the River Tedjen now irrigates two oases: the Serakhs Oasis and the Tedjen Oasis, and even now, during seasonal inundations, the waters of this river extend far into the Kara Kum Desert. Special geomorphological studies have shown that in prehistoric times the Gerirud-Tedjen had a large delta made up of a multitude of wide channels. These channels were flanked by lush vegetation which created highly favourable conditions for irrigation farming in very ancient times.

An analysis of charcoal excavated in the settlements of the Geoksyur Oasis shows that poplar, *karagach,* maple, tamarisk and other deciduous trees grew near the delta streams. This brushwood provided good raw material which the inhabitants of the Geoksyur Oasis exploited with success in building and other everyday needs. The ancient river delta had fertile alluvial soil which gave high crop yields. It has been suggested that when the oases of the foothills of the Kopet Dag mountains had been settled and all the land suitable for cultivation was being exploited, the surplus population was forced to colonize the Tedjen Delta and other areas.

The Geoksyur Oasis is believed to have been settled by people from settlements of the Kara-depe/Namazga-depe type in the central area; the fact that Anau I–Namazga I layers become thinner in the more easterly settlements bears this out. For example, in the northern mound at Anau the relevant layer is 12 m. thick, but further east, at Kara-depe, it is 6.5 m., at Namazga-depe 6 m. and in the Geoksyur Oasis never thicker than 2–2.5 m. The discovery in south-eastern Turkmenia of Neolithic (Djeitun culture) settlements such as Chagilli and villages of the early Chalcolithic period (Mondjukli, Chakmakli) indicates with a fair degree of certainty that it was the local eastern Anau groups which colonized the Tedjen delta.

In any case, it is now quite clear that this fertile oasis, far from the Kopet Dag mountains, was settled late in the Namazga I period. Of the nine Chalcolithic settlements uncovered so far, only the lower levels of the settlements of Geoksyur I, Yalangach-depe, Akcha-depe and all the levels of Dashlidji-depe belong to the period in question, the excavations of Dashlidji-depe giving an especially full picture of the settlements. It is a very small settlement (45 m. × 38 m. × 2 m.), with 3 building levels excavated all the way down to the underlying alluvial deposits. All the structures were made of sunbaked bricks. The village comprises living and domestic areas which form separate independent complexes. Each living room has an area of 6–12 sq. m. with a threshold containing a stone door-socket, and a rectangular hearth on the left of the entrance. In front of each house is a small courtyard with subsidiary structures probably for storage. This arrangement bears a strong resemblance to the house-building principles of the Djeitun culture. All the rooms of Dashlidji-depe are small except for one, which has an area of 28.5 sq. m. It has a couch next to the wall, a rectangular hearth in the corner and its floor was painted in black and red. The room was possibly used as a shrine although in all other respects it is no different from the rest of the rooms. At the edge of the settlement traces of a pottery production area have been observed. In addition, there were in this area straight parallel low walls which could have been used for sun-drying meat and corn. This description is typical of a small village of the Anau I–Namazga I period, and other villages of the Geoksyur Oasis, and possibly of the whole of southern Turkmenia, were very similar. On the other hand, the central settlement of Geoksyur I in this period covered a much larger area, although it is still difficult to reconstruct its plan.

The painted pottery of this period from the Geoksyur Oasis is largely the same as the decorated ware from the foot-hills. There are, however, some differences, for example the preference for light shades for the burnished slip and the use of such painted patterns as triangular chevrons, horizontal zigzags and parallel arches along the rim.

The anthropomorphic figurines of Geoksyur also have distinctive features. Here, just as at Kara-depe, the female figurines were portrayed in a standing position, but they are much more schematized. One of the figurines from Dashlidji has survived complete; it was modelled without arms or breasts; its blurred facial contours are completely dominated by a large nose, all the other features being indicated merely by shallow depressions. This highly conventionalized plaque style of figurine from Dashlidji-depe which is in sharp contrast to the realistically portrayed female figurines from Kara-depe, may also be the result of influence from south-west Iran. The cylindrical bases of figurines from the Geoksyur Oasis and Suziana are significant in this respect. The majority of zoomorphic figurines represent goats and sheep rather than bovids and horses.

Great qualitative changes are noticeable also in the economy. In the osteological material from Dashlidji-depe twenty-two individuals were identified as cattle and small domesticated animals (including pig) but only six as onager, gazelle and wild sheep. Thus hunting clearly played a subsidiary role compared to the breeding of domesticated animals which provided meat, wool and milk. It is no accident, therefore, that at Dashlidji over fifty spindle-whorls have been found, while bone tools used for working skins have almost completely disappeared. The wool of domesticated animals and the yarn which was produced from it replaced the skin clothing of the preceding Neolithic period. Thus the formation of a settled farming economy and culture was complete. This direction of progress and prosperity gradually embraced all the early prehistoric farmers in southern Turkmenia, especially in the middle Chalcolithic period, corresponding to the archaeological complex of Anau II.

MIDDLE CHALCOLITHIC PERIOD: NAMAZGA II

The middle Chalcolithic period is characterized by polychrome decoration of pottery. At Namazga-depe it is represented in the assemblage of Namazga II. It was now that the uniformity of the southern Turkmenian culture began to dissolve. Thus, in the western and central areas the monochrome painted decoration of the pottery of the Anau I–Namazga I period was replaced by bright polychrome friezes made up of small geometric figures on a light, predominantly cream or yellowish ground. Occasionally drawings of goats and even people were portrayed in an exaggeratedly stylized manner.

Fig. 15

This culture was found in layers ranging in thickness between 2.5 and 6 m. in the settlements of Tilkin-depe, the northern mound of Anau, Kara-depe, Elen-depe, and Namazga-depe. Polychrome decoration of pottery was long considered to be the basic character of the Namazga

Fig. 15   Polychrome painted pottery of Namazga II type

Fig. 16
Plate 12

II complex. However, the establishment of a more detailed stratigraphy for Kara-depe has proved this assumption wrong. On this site, in an excavated area of 20 × 20 m., six building levels designated Kara 1–6 have been distinguished. The Kara 2–6 levels belong completely to the Namazga II culture. This culture spans the period between the emergence of polychrome ware and the evolution of monochrome zoomorphic motifs which continue into the next period, Namazga III. In addition the establishment of the stratigraphy according to building levels provides the basis of the subdivision of Namazga II into an early and late phase.

The early phase is represented by Kara 4, 5 and 6. These levels contain remains of houses made of sun-dried bricks and traces of pottery production, possibly using a kiln.

Polychrome decoration is found on 62% of all the pottery, whereas the monochrome painted pottery forms only about 10%. The undecorated pottery includes red-slipped hemispherical bowls, often highly burnished, while the amount of polished grey ware is much smaller. The coarse ware consists mainly of large vessels and round bowls.

In the overlying subsequent level (Kara 3) living and domestic rooms of sun-dried brick have been uncovered. Both the floor and the walls were coated with clay plaster, and in some places the floor was also brick-laid. The stone door socket near the threshold is a common feature of many living rooms. The storerooms had large pithos-shaped vessels dug into the earth; where their floors were covered with broken pottery, it was most likely for protecting grain from the damp. A preponderance of monochrome ware over polychrome ware forms the basis of assigning the Kara 3 level to the late phase of Namazga II.

The next level, Kara 2, also belongs to the final phase. Here, structures built of sun-dried bricks were excavated. The structures in this level have been tentatively grouped into two or three building complexes

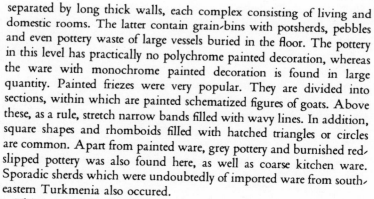

Fig. 16   *Monochrome painted pottery of Namazga II type*

separated by long thick walls, each complex consisting of living and domestic rooms. The latter contain grain-bins with potsherds, pebbles and even pottery waste of large vessels buried in the floor. The pottery in this level has practically no polychrome painted decoration, whereas the ware with monochrome painted decoration is found in large quantity. Painted friezes were very popular. They are divided into sections, within which are painted schematized figures of goats. Above these, as a rule, stretch narrow bands filled with wavy lines. In addition, square shapes and rhomboids filled with hatched triangles or circles are common. Apart from painted ware, grey pottery and burnished red-slipped pottery was also found here, as well as coarse kitchen ware. Sporadic sherds which were undoubtedly of imported ware from south-eastern Turkmenia also occured.

This sequence is also characteristic of the pottery of such settlements as Anau and Namazga-depe. Further discoveries may provide some basis by which it will be possible to differentiate the pottery of each individual settlement.

The formation of the Namazga II culture has been debated for a long time in archaeological circles. For example, G. Schmidt considered that this polychrome pottery lay outside the general local pottery develop-ment and seemed to be imported from some higher cultural centre. Later, McCowan and Piggott linked its origin with Baluchistani influence on Anau. Another view is that the Namazga II culture is basically of local origin, although its source has not yet been traced either to southern Turkmenia or Iranian Khorasan. At the same time certain parallels have been established with the pottery decoration from Djovi, in south western Iran which indicate the direction of cultural contacts although they by-passed the oases of Central and Northern Iran (Sialk-Hissar).

The most recent excavations at Tali Iblis provided additional information, although still insufficient to solve the problem. Thus, at site 'S', in level IV, polychrome pottery was found, which in a number of cases was similar to that from southern Turkmenia. In Tali Iblis, however, this would seem to have no local origin. According to some authorities, the stylistic similarities of pottery from Southern Iran, Pakistan and Southern Turkmenia proves the existence of prehistoric relationships between these large areas of the ancient Near East.

All the known burials of this period comprise inhumations lying in a contracted position facing south. A systematic excavation of the Kara-depe site has shown that its inhabitants buried their fellow tribesmen in derelict wasteland on this huge settlement. There is no evidence of a permanent cemetery area. On the contrary, these temporarily abandoned areas were later used for house-building so that the former burials lay under the floors of new houses. Thus the burials found in the Kara 3 level belong to the inhabitants of the Kara 2 level, and so on. Some burial pits cut through walls built years before but there is no direct incontestible evidence of ritual burials under the floors of inhabited rooms. This, however, does not exclude the possibility that ritual burial of children was practiced. The burial pits were often lined with bricks, as in Kara-depe, where one of the pits was even divided into two chambers with a brick partition. Occasionally the bodies were wrapped in reed mats or sprinkled with ochre. One burial pit contained three bodies lying next to each other.

Thirty-five burials were excavated in the Kara 2 level. The most common burial position, recorded in twenty-two cases, was for the body to be laid on its right side in a contracted position, the extended right arm close into the body, and the left bent at the elbow. In isolated cases both arms were stretched along the body. The grave-goods comprised mostly necklaces and bracelets. Outstanding in this respect is the burial of a child of some 12–15 months, with a necklace round its neck and azurite beads at its knees. These beads could have been sewn on to a robe or a coat. Only one burial, that of an old woman, contained a vessel.

The Kara 3 level contained twenty-one burials. According to their position they may be divided into two groups; both lay on the right side, the first group with the right arm straight and the left arm bent; the other group with both arms stretched beside the body. As in the Kara 2 level, grave-goods were found in only half the burials and consisted of a similar set of ornaments. Here again a child's burial merits special attention, for next to its skeleton were found 420 gypsum beads, as well as one of carnelian, two of azurite and six of gypsum wrapped in silver foil. On the wrists the child had bracelets made of carnelian and azurite, and even a gold bead, the oldest so far discovered in Western Central Asia.

The metal artifacts used by the inhabitants of the foot-hills of the Kopet Dag in the middle Chalcolithic period were insignificant. They include small pins with pyramidal heads, and an ornament of twisted wire from Anau. The collection includes a small number of metal tools (awls) and a spear-head, also from Anau. The metal content of a large piercer from Kara-depe has been analysed: 98% copper, 1% lead, 0.1% nickel and 0.05% iron. The small number of metal tools can be explained by the absence of local ore deposits. For this reason broken metal artifacts were never thrown away but, as was suggested by Gordon Childe, were re-smelted.

It is significant, however, that flint tools are not very numerous either— they include isolated blades, probably used as sickle inserts. Sandstone and limestone were used in the manufacture of querns, mortars and pounders. A relatively large number of stone rings has been found which it has been suggested were for weighting digging-sticks.

Anthropomorphic figurines are unfortunately represented by only a few poorly-preserved examples. It is significant that all the figurines are modelled in a sitting position, a previously unknown iconographic feature in this region. The meaning of painted zigzags on the hips of some of the figurines has not been established. One figurine has a goat painted on its hips in the same schematic style as the goats painted on the pottery of the late Namazga II culture. In the Kara 2 level, at Kara-depe, one of the most ancient figurines of a man has been found; he is shown bearded and in a seated position. Among the material of the Kara 3 level a heavy model wheel with a projecting hub was found, possibly from a miniature model of a cart.

The Middle Chalcolithic saw the emergence of two historico-cultural areas—eastern and central. In contrast to the central area, where pottery was decorated with polychrome friezes, in the eastern area the old ceramic style continued, with only minor changes.

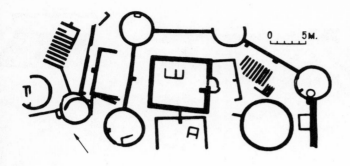

THE YALANGACH PERIOD

Fig. 18
Plate 11

The complete range of this pottery was excavated in the settlement of Yalangach-depe in the Geoksyur Oasis, the Yalangach period in the history of this area being the time when the population of the Geoksyur Oasis was at its largest. Apart from Dashlidji-depe, which had been abandoned by this time, eight other settlements still existed here—Yalangach, Mullali, Aina, Akcha, Chong, Geoksyur VII, Geoksyur IX, Geoksyur I. Thus the number of villages in the oasis was double that of the preceding period. This can be explained only by internal processes in the development of society and in general the Geoksyur Oasis provides—in a way in which no other oasis in southern Turkmenia can—the key to the reconstruction of these historical and cultural processes in the fourth-early third millennia BC. Here, away from the densely populated foot-hills of the Kopet Dag, a small, relatively isolated, enclave of people was founded. The basic stages in their development reflect in miniature the socio-historical development of Turkmenia, something much more difficult to perceive in the large and once thickly-populated settlements in the south of the country.

The largest settlement in the Yalangach period, and probably also in earlier periods, was Geoksyur I, whose area had by now increased to 25 acres. Unfortunately the relevant levels were buried deep under layers of the late Chalcolithic period, with limited accessibility through trial trenches and small excavations. Thus the general plan of this central settlement of the Yalangach period is still not very clear. Small excavations carried out on the edge of the site revealed traces of a defensive wall and a round-based tower. It is difficult to tell whether in the Yalangach period Geoksyur I was surrounded by a wall all along its perimeter as

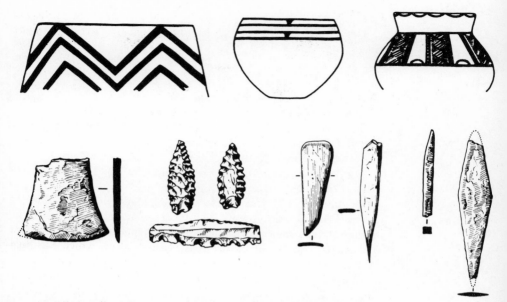

were certain smaller villages, or whether only separate residential sections were walled. It is certain, however, that there were two types of settlement in the Geoksyur Oasis: small rural groups and the 'capital', Geoksyur I. There may have been a similar situation during the preceding Dashlidji period, but this is still conjectural.

Settlements such as Yalangach-depe and Mullali-depe were excavated over the entire area of the site to a depth of the second and third building levels. This, in turn, clarified the general development of building principles in each settlement. Yalangach-depe is a small mound about 5 m. high and with an area of 130 m. ×95 m. Two building levels have been horizontally excavated. In the top level an encircling wall with round towers was excavated, and within this wall two rooms with two-tiered ovens (podiums) were partially exposed. A round structure filled with pieces of charred brick was also found. In the lower building level, two apparently independent complexes divided by a thick wall were excavated. In the eastern section of the site, structures continued to consist of a central room with a number of smaller adjoining rooms. The eastern complex was possibly used as a shrine, while the western complex was made up of dwellings. Although no encircling walls

Fig. 17

have been found in this level, their existence should not be completely ruled out; if they originally stood at the edge of the village, they may have been eroded away later. Indirect evidence of this may be found in the plan of another settlement—Mullali-depe: the outer, better preserved edge of this site had an encircling wall with round towers, which means that the whole village could have been surrounded by a defensive wall.

The other settlements of the Yalangach period are similar to those described above. Besides the dwelling places, the villages had shrines containing podiums. These were made of clay, and were divided in the interior into two parts, one part usually bearing traces of burning. In the village of Akcha-depe the raised edge that formed the podium had short pillars at the corners, with a broken cup in one of the two sections. These supposed shrines seem very modest, and only the podium, which may have served as a kind of altar, indicates their function.

In two villages—Akcha-depe and Geoksyur—remains of ancient ditches have been excavated round the outer side of the defensive wall.

As mentioned earlier, the villages of the Neolithic and the early Chalcolithic periods consisted as a rule of one-roomed houses. Detached separate houses with subsidiary structures have also been found in the villages of the Yalangach period, but in this period there was a tendency for their unification into agglomerated residential areas. This process reached its climax in the late Chalcolithic period. The evidence of this evolution of village planning is based mainly on the material excavated in the Geoksyur Oasis and does not necessarily hold true for the whole of southern Turkmenia. During the late Chalcolithic period, however, multi-roomed houses were universal from Geoksyur to Kara-depe. It would seem that these architectural modifications reflect changes that were taking place in society, for instance, in the evolution from the nuclear families of the Neolithic period to extended family communities of the Chalcolithic.

There is no need to exaggerate the importance of the fortress walls. Separated from their metropolis in the foothills, the inhabitants of the oasis had to protect themselves from possible attack. There is no evidence, however, that these tiny villages had accummulated wealth enough to tempt invaders. The material excavated here shows that they were a series of ordinary sedentary agricultural villages with a crude set of equipment typical of rural settlers. In fact, apart from the modestly decorated pottery, small clay figurines and domestic implements there is nothing of any value at these sites, the only luxury items being a few ornaments made of carnelian, turquoise, agate and azurite. This is not to say that the community suffered from social or economic stagnation; on the contrary, it was a time of rapid progress within the framework of the sedentary agricultural system. It is interesting to note in this connection the discovery of flint sickle blades with denticulated cutting edges; stone mortars, querns and pounders have also been found in large numbers. In addition, metal tools increased considerably in variety, and now included a heavy axe, spear-heads and what may be a razor. An analysis of these objects shows that they were manufactured not from native copper but from copper ore, using a rather complicated annealing technique which increased the hardness of the metal. Bone tools, comprising in the main awls, piercers and a possible borer, also occurred. Carbonised grains of *Hordeum distichum* (two-row barley) and *Triticum vulgare* (wheat) were also found here. The proportion of barley to wheat is roughly 30:1 and analogous ratios found in other settlements of southern Turkmenia, such as Namazga-depe, for example, prove the predominance of barley over wheat in this period. The role of hunting was reduced to a minimum, which is reflected in the fact that the bones of domesticated animals account for 90% of the total osteological material; of these, goats and sheep predominate over cattle in a ratio of 1:7. The bones of wild animals which have been found are mostly those of horse, gazelle, Western Central Asian deer, boar and fox (the last three lived in thick brushwood).

The collection of figurines from the Geoksyur Oasis is unexpectedly large: about 100 fragments of female figurines. At Yalangach-depe a complete figurine 28 cm. long was found, giving a good idea of the iconography of the female deity. It shows a woman in a sitting position, her head slightly tilted back and her facial features very schematized, with round holes for eyes and black-painted eyebrows. Two broad painted bands round the neck may represent ornaments. Below these, in front, three rows of dotted lines form a kind of necklace. The figurine has no arms, the emphasis being on the full breasts with black nipples. The thighs are painted with circles dotted on the inside possibly in imitation of the sun, and the pubic region was indicated by a painted triangle. The artist undoubtedly sought to convey the image of a fertile

Plate 10
Fig. 19

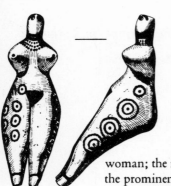

Fig. 19   Figurines of the Namazga II period, from Yalangach-depe

woman; the mother goddess. What strikes the eye first is the full breasts, the prominent stomach and fat thighs, while all the other details seem to be of little importance. Most of the female figurines resemble the one described above. The main difference is in the size (up to 10–12 cm. high) and in some of the details of the painting with, for example, goats being painted on the hips instead of the sun. Some figurines have their arms folded on their stomachs, with the hands cupped under the breasts. This general iconographic image of a sitting female goddess, with certain variations, survived until the end of the second millennium BC over the entire territory of southern Turkmenia.

It would be wrong to think that the people of the Geoksyur Oasis were completely isolated and maintained no contact with the groups in the foothills of the Kopet Dag. Evidence of contact may be seen in the presence of bright polychrome painted sherds in the mass of the poorly decorated pottery. These were painted red and black on a cream or yellowish ground; the typical ware of the early Namazga II culture used by the inhabitants of the oases in the foot-hills of the Kopet Dag mountains. The similarity is so striking that there is no doubt as to the origin of those sherds. They are decorated with friezes of people, trees and even fantastic creatures of mixed human, arboreal and avian elements. It is this category of pottery that makes it possible to establish the approximate chronological limits of the Yalangach period within Anau II–Namazga II in the central zone.

An important small group of monochrome pottery, decorated with large hatched and cross-hatched rhomboidal and triangular patterns can be distinguished by its shapes and decoration from the mass of pottery recovered in Geoksyur and has its analogies in distant Mesopotamia. It may be observed not only at the Geoksyur Oasis but in all the corresponding cultural layers of settlements in south-eastern Turkmenia.

Finally, very few burials have been found in the villages of the Yalangach period; on the other hand, in the central settlement of Geoksyur I they occur fairly frequently. The most logical explanation of this is that the small villages had no convenient places for cemeteries whereas at Geoksyur I there was always abandoned land suitable for this purpose. In any case no graves have been found outside the villages, nor is there any evidence of cremation. This, in turn, serves as indirect proof that the fortified villages were not isolated from one another, but, on the contrary, formed a unified whole, so that the entire Geoksyur oasis in this period formed a closely-knit community.

The Yalangach period is not confined to the boundaries of the Geoksyur Oasis. It may be observed as a historico-cultural phase in other settlements of south-eastern Turkmenia. For example, in the cross-section at Iilginli-depe, stratified directly over the Anau I–Namazga I layer, was a layer 5 m. thick containing an assemblage of the Yalangach period. Trial excavations and surface collections have revealed analogous assemblages in such 'capitals' as Altin-depe and Ulug-depe, a border settlement near Dushak. West of it is the central area where the equivalent of the Yalangach period—the Namazga II period—predominated at Kara-depe and Namazga-depe and at a number of smaller settlements.

As may be seen, the amount of information about the cultural level of the central area of southern Turkmenia is much greater than that of the eastern area. So far the main cultural distinction, superficial as it might be, is between the pottery. This and other indirect evidence indicates beyond any doubt that the once uniform culture began to split into two distinct ethnio-cultural zones. This separation, however, is not reflected in the agricultural-stockbreeding economy typical of the whole of southern Turkmenia.

Thus, in the fifth-fourth millennia BC, southern Turkmenia was a prosperous country of agricultural oases, with developed architecture, gaily coloured pottery and superb figurines. All these achievements are particularly striking when compared with the other parts of Western Central Asia, where at this time the archaic Neolithic culture still predominated. It would seem that hunting, fishing and food-gathering, which were the chief activities of these local groups, retarded the general economic progress so that the inhabitants of the northern parts of the country were outstripped by their south-western contemporaries.

Central Asia

Thanks to the extensive research carried out in the north of Turkmenia it has been possible to isolate a number of industries and cultures character istic of this northern Neolithic. Many Neolithic sites were discovered to the east of the Caspian Sea, and particularly in the area of Kara Bogaz (Hodja Su, Chaganak, Djanak, and some others). These sites had a distinct assemblage of tools: large elongated blades, micro-blades, cutters, large trapezes and numerous pointed scrapers. The total absence of pottery points to the archaic nature of these assemblages.

Valuable material has been excavated in the territory of the Great Balk-han Desert (Bash Keriz, Tash Arvat), in which tools made of flakes were very common, primarily scrapers and burins. No micro-blades or geometric microliths were found. The site at Oyukli, in the North Balkhan Desert, has produced an even more distinctive collection of artifacts including pointed scrapers, cutters, notched blades and backed micro-blades alongside round-based vessels with incised decoration. These variations very possibly reflect a certain ethnical departure from the Caspian groups in the Neolithic period.

The most important sites of the Caspian area are the caves of Djebel and Dam-Dam-Chashma 2 which show a clear sequence of cultural levels dating back to the Mesolithic deposits. The fourth level of Djebel (4070± 140 BC) contains round-based pottery with incised decoration, which was different from the decoration of the Oyukli ware. Also found here were notched blades, scrapers, trapezoids and arrow-heads of two kinds: leaf-shaped and hollowed on one side. Sea-shells and beads were the only ornaments in this assemblage. Similar beads were found in the Neolithic burials near the Kailiu cave, in which there were also traces of ochre. In addition to the hand-made pottery already mentioned, the upper layers of the Djebel cave contained sporadic sherds of grey ware which were possibly imported from the sedentary agricultural settlements which existed in more southern regions in the third millennium BC. Judging from the osteological material recovered from the caves of Djebel and Dam-Dam-Chashma 2, their inhabitants subsisted mainly on fish and gazelle meat. It is possible that the Dam-Dam-Chashma 2 inhabitants domesticated goats as far back as the Late Mesolithic period, while the querns from the Djebel cave may have been used for grinding some kind of grain. To a certain extent this indicates the rise of a production economy. In any case, the hypothetical transition to a new type of economy did not lead to any results of the kind observed in the mixed economy of the Djeitun culture.

THE KELTEMINAR CULTURE

In contrast to the Caspian area, most of Central Asia in the Neolithic period was dominated by the stable Kelteminar culture. In this vast cultural area which covered many regions of Western Central Asia and Kazakhstan, local variants have been isolated which may have corresponded to different population groups. These include the so-called Akcha-Daryan group of sites (in the lower course of the River Amu Darya), the Tuzkan group (the lower course of the River Zeravshan), and the Uzboian group (along the ancient river bed that crosses the Kara Kum desert). The Kysyl Kum and the west Kazakhstan variants of the Kelteminar culture are characteristic of both the steppe and the desert zones. It is important to note here that the Kelteminar sites show traces of contact with the Neolithic culture of the Urals and western Siberia and possibly with the agricultural communities of south-western Central Asia.[2] Round-based and pointed-based pots, richly decorated with incised and stamped patterns were characteristic of the early Kelteminar sites. Many of the flint arrow-heads were frequently hollowed, and large numbers of trapezoid microliths were also found. The late Kelteminar culture is distinguished by globular vessels with flat bases. They are decorated much less lavishly and many vessels are undecorated. The flint implements consist of bifacial arrow-heads and a large number of spear-heads. Also in the later period there is evidence of the use of copper. This culture most likely existed from the fifth to the late third/early second millennia BC.

The location of the Kelteminar settlements on the banks of lakes, creeks and small streams could be explained by the importance of fishing in this period. It is not surprising that sinkers from nets, composite harpoons and fish hooks were excavated on these sites. Hunting for red deer, boar, roe deer, onager and wild horse was also of great importance to the people who lived in the lower course of the River Zeravshan; that food-gathering was still widely practised may be inferred from the numerous finds of land- and fresh-water mollusca. The late Kelteminar material, from the Tuzkan group of sites for example, includes sickle blades, querns and pounders, all of which point to the importance of food-gathering and possibly to the beginnings of agriculture. The bones of domesticated animals were also found.

Recent discoveries in Fergana show that this valley had a local Neolithic culture (the sites of Sarik Su, Bakhrabad and others) with a very marked microlithic set of tools, including micro-scrapers, piercers, and more rarely, lunates and trapezes. Although no pottery was found, sporadic sickle blades seem to point to some food-gathering.

THE HISSAR CULTURE

The picture is quite different in the eastern part of Western Central Asia, with its mountainous terrain. The Hissar culture, which predominated here, was characterized by crude pebble tools. These sites have been found mostly in Tadjikistan, although some may yet be discovered in Fergana and Kirghizia. The Hissar culture is dated tentatively to the sixth–early second millennia BC; its sites are located mostly along small rivers and streams, and on the terraces of big rivers (the sites of Kun Bulien, Tutkaul, and Seyed). The most complete sequence of cultural levels has been excavated at the site of Tutkaul, where stone-lined floors, some occupying as much as 40 sq. m., were found. They probably originally provided the foundation of reed huts. The second level at Tutkaul has a radiocarbon date of 5150 ± 140 BC. Although most of the implements were made from crudely flaked pebbles, there were also blade implements of flint, including trapezes and lunates. Other artifacts include arrow-heads, polished axes, pounders, mortars and granite querns; the only bone implements were piercers. Some of the sites produced coarse hand-made vessels with pointed bases, some of them with textile impressions. The economy of the Hissar culture is still not clear. The thick occupation layers (at Tutkaul) may hint at the existence of primitive agriculture and stock-breeding, but the basic equipment and the general aspect of the culture point to the predominance of a food-gathering economy.

We have ascertained, then, that the inhabitants of the south-west during this period had developed an economy based on agriculture, while the rest of the vast territory was inhabited by people who combined hunting and fishing with food-gathering and incipient stock-breeding, thus giving an archaic aspect to the Neolithic culture which dominated the huge territorial expanses of Western Central Asia and Kazakhstan.

CHAPTER VI

Turkmenia and Iran: Movements and Connections, 3000–2500 BC

During the Late Chalcolithic period, the early agricultural communities of southern Turkmenia made great cultural advances: the irrigation system was improved, the decoration of painted pottery grew more refined, and figurines of high quality were produced, while at the same time there were increasing contacts with the settlements of neighbouring countries.

NAMAZGA III

Archaeological findings suggest that the Late Chalcolithic is character/ized by the Namazga III culture which was discovered by Kuftin in the village of Namazga/depe. As already mentioned, the incipient ethno/cultural independence of southern Turkmenia in the central and eastern regions was already established rather earlier, in the period of Namazga II. During the Namazga III period (from the fourth to the first half of the third millennium BC) these regions attained a still greater degree of cultural independence with a tentative border passing, as before, through the village of Ulug/depe.

To understand the nature of these changes, we shall first examine the sites of the central zone. Here the preceding ceramic style of the late Namazga II period (layers Kara 3–2 at Kara/depe) was being replaced by an essentially new zoomorphic type of decoration.

To date, the pottery of the Namazga III culture found at Kara/depe, where the layers of that period are 2.5 m. thick, has been most intensively studied. The entire ceramic material from Kara/depe falls into two main groups: fine ware and coarse (kitchen) ware. The first group includes painted ware with a light or, more rarely, red background; polychrome painting and plain grey ware are rare. The pottery featuring zoomorphic motifs is more spectacular but occurs less frequently than that with geometric patterns, the monochrome painted ware with geometric patterns predominating in Kara/depe as well as at other villages of this period. This comprises mainly deep bowls, but ribbed bowls, hemis/pherical bowls, basins, biconical vessels and shallow plates decorated

Plates 16–21, 23

75

in this manner are also found. As a rule, the upper part of the vessel is adorned with a wide band of geometric patterns of intricate design. A large number of them undoubtedly reflect the influence of the ceramic art of south-eastern Turkmenia (so-called Geoksyur style) although in a modified form.

The red-slipped ware hardly differs in its forms from the light-slipped ware, though no zoomorphic patterns have yet been found on it.

There are only a few examples of polychrome pottery from the upper layer of Kara-depe. This small yet rather expressive group of pottery has no local prototypes, but bears a definite resemblance to the Mesopotamian ware of the Jemdet-Nasr period. As in the preceding period, the plain ware from Kara-depe is mostly grey, sometimes burnished with incised ornaments.

Although, as we have seen, the Namazga II ceramic complex at Kara-depe belongs to the earlier phase, the ceramic material of the corresponding layers at Gara-depe (near Koushut) and at Namazga-depe seems to differ very little and on the whole fits in with the characteristics of the Namazga III ware.

Even the first published descriptions of the Late Chalcolithic pottery helped establish its connection with the contemporary pottery found at Sialk III 4–7 and Hissar Ic-IIa. Subsequent accumulation of material has provided additional evidence of this connection.

Thus, the drawings of heraldic eagles on the pottery from Kara-depe, though not known in Hissar, have been found in Sialk III4 and go back to similar motifs in south-western Iran. The same holds true for the pictures of cows and birds, analogies of which have been found again at such sites in Iran as Sialk III and Giyan V. It should be noted that all these new motifs of the Namazga III ware were completely unknown here earlier. In this case the comparisons mentioned above give considerable support to the hypothesis that early in the third millennium BC southern Turkmenia was invaded by tribes from northern Iran. This is also borne out by certain changes in the burial rites. For example, at Kara-depe in the Namazga II period bodies were most commonly laid on the left side oriented towards the south, while during the Namazga III period, in addition to the above-mentioned features in the burial ritual, there were substantial anthropological changes which brought them closer to the type of people who inhabited Sialk and Hissar.

As a result of excavations at Yarim-tepe, in the Gorgān Valley, North Iran, we are now able to assess the nature of this intrusion, since the cultural layers discovered here contained an assemblage of Namazga III culture. Thus it is possible to trace a whole chain of ancient settlements which indicate the diffusion of the Sialk-Hissar group of tribes *via* Yarim-tepe down to the submontane central zone of southern Turkmenia.

The top layer excavated at Kara-depe belongs entirely to the Namazga III period. In this layer a large empty area was discovered, which may have been a central square into which ran narrow lanes separating large multi-roomed houses. Sometimes these houses were separated from each other by thick fences.

Each house had living rooms with small hearths and adjacent auxiliary domestic structures and 'storage bins' whose walls and floors were faced with potsherds. Almost every house had its own inner courtyard. It seems likely that a multi-roomed house like this could have accommo-dated six to eight families united by kinship and economic ties. A rough estimate puts the entire population of Kara-depe in the Namazga III period at 1,000–1,600 people, although not all of the settlement was in-habited at that time, some of its sections having been abandoned back in the Namazga II period and never re-settled.

It would seem that Kara-depe was quite a large village for the Late Chalcolithic period, with a well-conceived plan. A characteristic feature was that special places had been set aside for rubbish, usually at the edge of the occupation zone. Despite the fact that a large area has been un-covered in the central section, no shrines have been found there.

On the other hand, the painted ware clearly shows that elaborate religious rites were practised here at that time. On one fragment, for example, can be discerned two human figures flanking an anthro-pomorphic deity which is a precise copy of the terracotta figurines dis-covered here. These predominantly female figurines, though few in number, are very significant. Although they have a certain iconographic unity, they differ stylistically. Some are executed in a relatively more realistic manner and have 'pinched' bird-like faces with slanting eyes and large noses; their heads are mostly adorned with complicated coiffures comprising small plaits, locks and S-shaped curls. The great majority are shown in sitting postures, with hands lowered. The most important figurine of this type came from a grave. Comparable figurines,

Plates 26–9

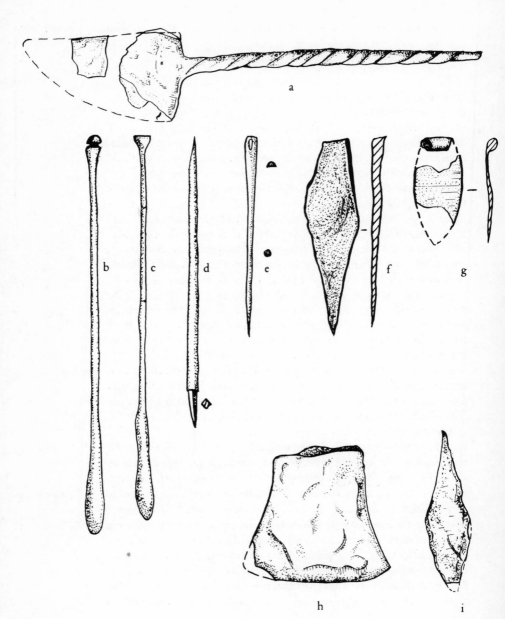

78

*Fig. 20 Some metal artifacts of the Chalcolithic period from southern Turkmenia.
a Mondjukli-depe; b, c, e Geoksyur I; d, j Kara-depe; f, h, i Yalangach-depe;
g Chakmakli-depe*

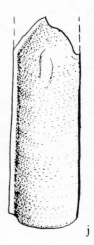

j

but without arms and breasts, as well as figurines without heads, are also found. At first glance the three types might reflect chronological stages in the schematization of anthropomorphic clay-modelling. However, the contexts in which they were found rule out such a possibility, for all of them were made more or less at the same time and were most likely associated with ancient magic and abstract thinking.

Male statuettes are sharply distinct from the general typology of female figurines. They occur only sporadically, but they are no less important. There are only three figurines of this kind found in the foot-hills of the Kopet Dag, all of them from the upper layer at Kara-depe. One of them, shown in a standing position, is known as the 'priest'. The second, of which only the skilfully fashioned head has been preserved, possibly represents the same type. The head is clad in a miniature helmet with occipital guards and cheek pieces, while down the back falls a serpentine plume. Another head, with broad features, aquiline nose and long neck, represents a rather different type. It is quite possible that the two heads reflect the ethnic types which actually existed in southern Turkmenia in the third millennium BC.

Plates 30, 31

The zoomorphic figurines found are relatively varied; most of them comprise conventionalized animal representations modelled in clay. Occasionally they bear painted patterns which may represent harness. The presence of numerous conical spindle-whorls provides convincing evidence of the extensive practice of weaving at this time.

Plate 24

It is in the Namazga III period that ceramic and stone amulets with carved geometric designs, perforated for suspension, appear for the first time. As before, the number of copper artifacts is small, and comprises awls and piercers, and a fragment of a knife or a chisel. The most wide-spread ornaments are long pins, some of them twisted, with roughly triangular, flat tips and thick butts, as well as simple bracelets and rings.

Plate 25

Fig. 20

The number of bone tools is also small. These include piercers and rods with polished tips which could have been used for mat-weaving.

At the same time wider use was made of stone vessels skilfully carved and chiselled out of pink or white alabaster. Some of them are decorated with incised ornaments and even have fluted sides. In addition to the

79

Plate 22

semi-precious stones out of which beads and pendants were fashioned, white alabaster was also commonly used for making ornaments. Beads, pendants and amulets of this material are generally found in burial pits. Larger artifacts have also been discovered, for example a bull statuette from Kara-depe.

The harder varieties of stone were used for making querns, pestles, mortars, 'weights', door sockets, and rounded objects with a circumferential groove. The latter closely resemble the balls found at Hissar-tepe which have been classified as 'hammers' or 'weights'.

Unfortunately, the layers containing material of the Namazga III period at other settlements of southern Turkmenia (e.g. Gara-depe) have only been probed with trial trenches so no new pertinent information has come from this source. These assemblages, together with the information obtained from Kara-depe, characterize the general pattern of development attained by local tribes in the first half of the third millennium BC. As in preceding periods large settlements existed alongside small ones. Notable changes took place in the interior planning of settlements, which now became more systematic, with large multiroomed houses, divided by 'streets' and lanes into 'blocks'. Each house had a number of living and work-rooms, as well as store-rooms, a courtyard and possibly a kitchen, suggesting that the community consisted of large families, or clans. There were, undoubtedly, some public governing bodies, which handled problems of general concern, and it is quite possible that the squares (like the one uncovered at Kara-depe) were used for public assemblies and festivities.

Although at this time in the Geoksyur Oasis there existed large villages such as Ulug-depe, Altin-depe, Iilginli-depe and many others, excavations at the Geoksyur I settlement have yielded the most extensive information. Just as at Kara-depe, the entire community here occupied separate multi-roomed dwellings divided by streets and thick walls. Each house consisted of an inner courtyard, workrooms and store-rooms, a smithy and possibly a family shrine with a round hearth in the centre. As a rule, such hearths consisted of a deep depression filled with ashes surrounded by a low baulk.

The established type of construction was not restricted to large villages such as Kara-depe and Geoksyur. Excavations in the small settlement of Chong-depe in the Geoksyur Oasis have removed any doubt of this.

In southern Turkmenia, the process of transition from one-roomed dwelling settlements of the Djeitun period to villages with multi-roomed houses was slightly impeded but not checked altogether by the infiltration of new tribal groups into the area. This is evident from the material of the Late Chalcolithic of south-eastern Turkmenia.

Research done at Altin-depe, Iilginli-depe and particularly the villages of the Geoksyur Oasis clearly points to an infiltration of newcomers in the fourth-third millennia BC. Significant in this respect is the material obtained from the stratigraphical trench sunk to a depth of 10 m. at Geoksyur I. It shows that one ceramic style was suddenly replaced by another. The many metres of cultural deposits from the very bottom of the shaft revealed a continuous genetic evolution of pottery styles from the Early Chalcolithic (Dashlidji period) to the Middle Chalcolithic (Yalangach period). In the late phase of the Yalangach period (the third building level from the top) painted pottery disappeared completely.

The material from the two uppermost building levels is especially interesting. Here there suddenly occurred richly-ornamented and elegant pottery of the so-called Geoksyur polychrome style. Despite the use of the bichrome decoration, this pottery has nothing in common with the polychrome ceramic painting of the early Namazga II period. It has, however, been found associated with sporadic sherds of monochrome ware typical of the late Anau II–Namazga II period of the Central zone.

A comparison of the stratified sections of Geoksyur and Kara-depe shows that the material of the building complex of Geoksyur II corresponds chronologically to the layer of Kara II in the village of Kara-depe. Furthermore, this correlation is supported by the discovery of sherds of what is obviously imported Geoksyur polychrome precisely in the Kara II layer, at the village of Kara-depe. Polychrome pottery appeared in the Geoksyur Oasis at the end of the Namazga II period, *i.e.* shortly before the zoomorphic ware spread to the central zone of southern Turkmenia.

Excavations in south-eastern Turkmenia show that this independent Geoksyur pottery style developed in the villages of Ulug-depe, Altin-depe, Serakhs and in most of the settlements of the Geoksyur Oasis. It lasted throughout the first half of the third millennium BC, *i.e.* it was

contemporary with the zoomorphic pottery of the Namazga III period. This correlation is again confirmed by the occurrence of sherds with zoomorphic decoration from south-eastern Turkmenia and by the imported Geoksyur ware of the Namazga III layers in the central area (Namazga-depe, Kara-depe, etc.).

As in the Middle Chalcolithic period, the border line between these two complexes ran between the villages of Kara-depe and Ulug-depe.

THE GEOKSYURIAN PERIOD

Figs. 21, 22

In the south-eastern area, this period may be designated 'Geoksyurian', as its identification rests solely on materials from the Geoksyur Oasis. In fact human settlement continued at that time only in two villages—Geoksyur I and Chong-depe, while the villages of Mullali-depe and Geoksyur IX were soon abandoned. This may give the impression that the Oasis site was reduced through an invasion by war-like tribes, with the result that out of the eight flourishing villages which had stood here in the Yalangach period only two survived. This convenient explanation, however, does not hold water. It has been proved that the deterioration of the Oasis began long before the diffusion of the Geok-

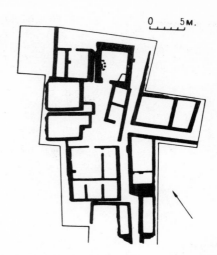

Figs 21, 22   Assemblage of Geoksyur type. Left, pottery, figurines and flints; above,
burial chamber and settlement type

syur ceramic style. In the later phase of the Yalangach period, only four
of the eight villages survived. This process of contraction was most likely
brought about by the old river *delta* shifting to the west.

That only two villages, Geoksyur I in the north and Chong-depe in
the south, remained by the end of the fourth millenium BC was possibly
due to the increasing concentration of the population in large villages.
On the whole the architecture and building methods of the Geoksyur
Oasis settlements are exactly the same as in the top level of Kara-depe.

Against this background the differences in pottery are particularly
noticeable. Although most of it is hand-made, some of the vessels seem
to have been wheel-turned. The pottery was fired in kilns of a rather
primitive design, two of which were exavated at the village of Geoksyur I.
They still have one tier, with the firing chamber separated from the
furnace by a partition.

The vessels are covered inside and out with a slip, mostly red or pink.
The friezes take up about three-quarters of the pots and consist of mixed
red-and black, sometimes only black, painted patterns. These patterns
are repeated at regular intervals and are separated by smaller patterns.
The most popular motif was one with large crosses enclosed in bright red

Plates 13, 14

83

polygons but others include Maltese crosses, rhomboids, triangles, bands with serrated edges, and chequers. On the whole the ceramic patterns of the Geoksyur Polychrome style are highly geometric and never show even a slightly curved line. Even the few zoomorphic representations are executed in an exaggeratedly geometric fashion. On many of the vessels straight lines run from the frieze down to the base, sometimes crossing in the middle of the base.

The most common forms of the painted ware are hemispherical bowls with flat bases and slightly concave rims. Less common are conical bowls, basins, biconical cups and pots, cylindrical vessels and spouted pots. Undecorated table ware was also produced, and comprises two groups—red-slipped and grey. The latter group is rare and consists of basins and pots, some of them burnished. The excavations at Geoksyur I yielded a grey-ware vase with a thin stem, the earliest of this kind found in southern Turkmenia.

As usual, the most numerous pots were those for domestic use—storage vessels, or *pithoi*, and rounded storage jars made of well-fired clay. Some of the *pithoi* have simple designs including crosses incised on the outer side of the rim.

The origin of the Geoksyur pottery style is still very obscure. Although a few of the decorative motifs have their prototypes in the ceramic painting of the preceding Namazga II period, on the whole this similarity is no more than superficial. The Geoksyur pottery is distinguished by its artistic taste and skilful workmanship, particularly when compared with the pottery of other places in southern Turkmenia. At the same time analogies have been established between this pottery and the painted ware of the adjacent areas of the Near East. No equivalents have been found in Mesopotamia, but the Buff Ware of south-western Iran closely resembles the Geoksyur polychrome pottery. At the same time, this pottery is very different from that of north-eastern Iran and most of southern Turkmenia. Thanks to the work of Stein, many important discoveries were made in southern Iran at the beginning of this century, some of which also shed light on the problem of the Geoksyur pottery style. Apart from identical designs, such as the Maltese crosses and certain other geometric patterns, the decoration of pottery bases is of particular interest. The lower part of the Geoksyur bowls is decorated by parallel lines that cross in the centre of the base, a feature which has an exact analogy in the ware of Tal-i-Bakun. The fact that not only individual motifs but also the very method of the Geoksyur ceramic decoration are similar to those of the Buff Ware culture points to a connection between the two. In turn, the Maltese cross of the Buff Ware culture has its analogies in the Samarra ware.

Setting aside the problem of the Mesopotamian or Iranian origin of the Samarra ware, these analogies of the Maltese cross in the form of goat figures on the Samarra painted pottery need not necessarily indicate that Buff Ware came directly from Mesopotamia. It would seem that it originated in the local Samarra-type ware of southern Iran.

Although there are apparent parallels between the pottery of the Geoksyur style and Buff Ware, no sites in the intervening areas have yet been discovered, which makes it difficult to establish a more definite relationship between them. It is clear, however, that at the end of the fourth millennium BC south-eastern Turkmenia was infiltrated by Iranian tribes possibly from the area of the Buff Ware culture. The newcomers brought their own ceramic styles which we have designated the Geoksyur polychrome pottery style.

The innovations were not limited to pottery-making, but spread to other cultural spheres as well, especially burial rites, family burials appearing in large chambers, alongside simple burial pits in the villages of south-eastern Turkmenia (Khapuz-depe, Altin-depe, Ulug-depe). In the Geoksyur I settlement more than 30 such burial chambers (*tholoi*) were excavated. These cemeteries were built in the abandoned sections of villages, mostly on their outskirts. Each cemetery consisted of four to six chambers. Almost all the *tholoi* are round in plan (a few are rectangular) with vaulted ceilings, and are made of sun-baked bricks. The burial chambers were built underground, but were clearly visible on the surface. A bricked-up opening at the side was the only entrance to the cemetery. Some of the cemeteries were separated from the nearby houses by long walls with passages. In the centre of most of the chambers lay an articulated human skeleton, while the bones of as many as eight or ten skeletons were piled in a heap by the wall. The arrangement of these skeletons shows that each body was initially placed in the centre of the grave but was later removed to other parts to make way for the next burial. As this process continued, the old graves became filled up and new tombs were built near or on top of the old ones. As a rule, the grave-

Plate 15
Fig. 22

goods were rather poor, consisting for the most part only of vessels and personal ornaments.

Although the study of the Geoksyur burial chambers is far from complete, some preliminary conclusions may be drawn. An anthropological examination of the dead in a small cemetery of four *tholoi* showed that 59% of those buried were women, 15% men and 26% children.

The question now arises whether the Geoksyurians had originally come from other settlements and retained their traditional burial customs in their new surroundings. Further analysis of the archaeological and palaeoanthropological material of the Geoksyurian cemeteries will be necessary before this can be finally determined. But it is reasonable to assume that the two sets of burial customs indicate the coexistence of local and imported burial traditions, and it seems likely that those buried in the chambers were mostly of south Iranian origin, while the descendants of local south Turkmenian tribes continued to bury their dead in simple graves. Collective burials were common not only in the ancient Near East but also in the Mediterranean area, but the closest analogues of the Geoksyur burial chambers come once again from the area of the Buff Ware culture. Although the round burial chambers of Geoksyur resemble the 'bread oven' structures of the tenth layer of Tepe Gawra, still closer analogies have been found in Suziana where, at the village of Ali Abad, near Musiana, rectangular bricklaid tombs containing collective burials have been discovered. At Suza itself collective burials, resembling those at Musiana, have been excavated.

Thus, despite the scanty information at our disposal, it is possible to conclude that the construction of burial chambers in southeastern Turkmenia is connected with the appearance here of people with Geoksyurstyle pottery. What is more, the sporadic burial chambers in villages in the Central Zone, such as Karadepe definitely indicate influence from the east.

Such collective burials imply a more complicated structure of local society and the existence of large clans as its nucleus. This would have been a new type of community, far more advanced than the nuclear families of the preceding period, and may be taken to represent a transition to protourban civilization.

The anthropomorphic figurines of the Geoksyur period changed to a far lesser extent. None of the changes, mainly stylistic, overstepped the limits of the local traditions of the Yalangach period. Just as during the entire fourth millennium BC, in the Geoksyur period south-eastern Turkmenia can easily be distinguished from the rest of the country by the abundance of its anthropomorphic figurines. It is sufficient to mention that the site of Geoksyur I alone yielded about three hundred figurines, compared to a mere thirty from Kara-depe. Unfortunately, almost all of them are in a very poor state of preservation.

The female figurines of south-eastern Turkmenia in this period may be divided into two types. The first type was more common in early Geoksyurian times, *i.e.* late fourth–early third millennium BC. These were relatively large female figurines (25–30 cm. tall). They were made of clay heavily tempered with finely chopped chaff and straw and their upper part was covered with a pink or, more rarely, red slip. All of them were modelled in a sitting position and are noted for their relatively realistic portrayal. Their heads often have elongated 'dolichocephalic' skulls, while their faces have characteristically large noses and have been treated in a highly schematic way. The long neck merges with the sloping shoulders which end in short stubby arms held close to the sides, while the narrow waist merges with broad hips from which the legs project forwards. Many figurines have painted eyebrows, painted neck-laces and other ornaments, and painted sexual attributes. There is one figurine of a mother with a baby painted on her stomach, its hands clutching her breast. Pictures of felines, similar to those on Geoksyur pottery, are sometimes found painted on the hips and thighs. On the whole, the figurines are very similar to their steatopygous counterparts from the Yalangach period of south-eastern Turkmenia.

The second, later group of statuettes includes highly stylized figurines, some 7–10 cm. tall, made of close-textured clay with no admixture. These are also all shown in a sitting position, their bird-like heads attached to long necks. They have no arms or breasts; fat hips swell from a narrow waist and taper into long legs. In some instances the head has been given a complicated coiffure.

There was also a small isolated group of female figurines with almost square shoulders decorated with applied strips of clay or little round protuberances. Their arms are either held at the sides or are folded on the stomach. The torso of one such figurine is decorated with numerous little applied bosses while the breasts are in the shape of animal heads.

The male figurines are few in number compared with the female ones but are individually more significant. Some of them look very much like the Kara-depe 'priest' but with little skull-caps and long beards parted into two tufts. Figurines of warriors were made out of clay pressed into little moulds and a bone 'fabricator' was then used to give them their final form. They have long beak-shaped noses, well-modelled almond-shaped eyes and flaring eye-brows. Their heads are decorated with miniature helmets with loop-shaped cheek-pieces. All the known heads of warriors look very much like that of the figurine of a warrior recovered from Kara-depe, the only difference being that the figurines of warriors found in south-eastern Turkmenia are either beardless or have beards parted into two tufts. The necks of some of the figurines are encircled by concentric applied bands of clay and the shoulders decorated with small oval protuberances.

The heads of the warriors have no local equivalents, nor are there analogies among the clay figurines anywhere else in the ancient Near East. Both the origin and the purpose of these figurines therefore remain obscure. Having appeared here in the first half of the third millennium BC they soon disappeared, and no figurines of this kind have been found in later assemblages.

The many anthropomorphic figurines recovered from the villages of south-eastern Turkmenia have direct and exact replicas in the clay figurines of the Central Zone, notably at Kara-depe. Their similarity makes it quite clear that this style was developed under the influence of the sculptural traditions of south-eastern Turkmenia.

The zoomorphic figurines, as a rule, were executed in such a schematic, generalized manner that is difficult to say which particular animals they represent. This traditional treatment may show that the zoomorphic figurines were not made by potters but were, rather, the products of a craft based on folklore. Many of them were found among the ruins of crumbling buildings of unbaked brick, and it is conceivable that they were set into the walls when these were being erected, to serve some magical purpose. However that may be, it is clear that the anthropo-morphic statuettes were not toys, but had some important cult meaning. This is indicated by the presence of an established canonical type of figurine with the emphasis on the female sexual attributes: even the most schematically modelled examples had a triangle scratched out below the stomach. Their cult significance is clearly indicated by the recovery of figurines of this type from many burials at Kara-depe and Geoksyur.

The many ornaments found, mostly beads and pendants, were made from gypsum and, more rarely, turquoise, azurite, sardonyx, quartzite, agate and chalcedony. The holes were bored from both sides, and the gypsum beads were sometimes wrapped in thin gold foil. The oval and square amulets, made of fired clay and stone, were decorated with geometrical incised designs and were perforated for suspension. Soft varieties of stone were used for making miniature vessels, harder varieties being used in the manufacture of door sockets, querns, mortars, pounders, whetstones, and weights with handles.

Copper objects, in the form of ornaments, especially pins with thick-ened butts, were quite frequently found in graves. They often indicate a deliberate admixture of silver. A copper disc recovered from one of the *tholoi* of Geoksyur I was very likely used as a mirror.

IRANO–MESOPOTAMIAN INFLUENCES

All this evidence confirms that during the Namazga III period southern Turkmenia was infiltrated by two waves of tribes from the territory of ancient Iran. Firstly, at the end of the fourth millennium BC, south-eastern Turkmenia was invaded by tribes associated with the distinctive Geoksyur pottery. Finding themselves in a familiar milieu of settled agriculturalists, the newcomers were soon assimilated by the local population. By way of evidence of this we have the anthropomorphic figurines which essentially continued the local traditions of the preceding Yalangach period. There is nothing to suggest that the infiltration was accompanied by any military action or violence.

Early in the third millennium BC the Central Zone was infiltrated by tribes which presumably came from villages of the Sialk-Hissar type. Just like their Geoksyurian predecessors, the newcomers at first adhered to their own burial customs as well as to the traditional zoomorphic decoration on their pottery. Apparently, some time at the end of the fourth and the beginning of the third millennium BC (the Jemdet Nasr period), the territory of ancient Iran was the scene of major tribal migrations which reached the fertile oases of southern Turkmenia. It is quite possible that this migration reflected the general historical situation in the Jemdet Nasr period when the formation of an early urban society was in progress. Ancient Iran, with its rich deposits of metal ores and building stone, held an attraction for the newly formed states and encouraged their expansionist tendencies in an easterly direction. Lack of written records makes it difficult to say exactly what happened, but the very fact that this period coincided with the infiltration of some of the Iranian tribes into southern Turkmenia could hardly be explained by a mere desire of the agricultural tribes to settle new lands. Whatever the reason, there is indisputable archaeological evidence that it was during the Namazga III period that southern Turkmenia established definite contacts with far-off Mesopotamia.[1] For example, in south-eastern Turkmenia a category of ware differing greatly from the rest of the pottery in shape and decoration—monochrome cross-hatched rhomboids or triangles—has been found in all the villages with Yalangach-type assemblages, alongside local pottery. Its nearest analogies are to be found in the pottery of the Ubaid period, excavated in layers XVII-XVIII at Gawra and especially in northern Syria. Pottery with similar painting from Sialk II represents an intermediate link between the northern Ubaid and Yalangach assemblages. The round vessels of the Yalangach period have no local prototypes either, but are directly analogous to those in northern Mesopotamia.

It is interesting to note that, whereas these parallels of the Yalangach period relate to northern Mesopotamia, in the subsequent Geoksyur period the cultural links are with southern Mesopotamia. The anthro-pomorphic figurines of the Namazga III period also have analogies in

Fig. 23

the Ubaid period in southern Mesopotamia: there is a clear iconographic relationship between these two areas. For example, the figurines of women with babies from Geoksyur I and southern Mesopotamia look very much alike. It is significant, too that although on most of the south Turkmenian figurines the arms do not extend beyond the elbows and hang down, there are some examples which have their hands folded on the stomach, which was very typical of the figurines of southern Ubaid.

The problem of the male figurines is rather more complicated. The Kara-depe 'priest' comes very close to the figurines from the Ubaid occupation levels of the village of Uruk, showing that the image of a standing human figure definitely originated in southern Mesopotamia. On the other hand, one example from Geoksyur I shows a man in a sitting position, which proves that the new iconographic influences were

Fig. 23 Figurines of southern Turkmenia and Mesopotamia. a–c, g–i southern Turkmenia; d–f, j–l Mesopotamia

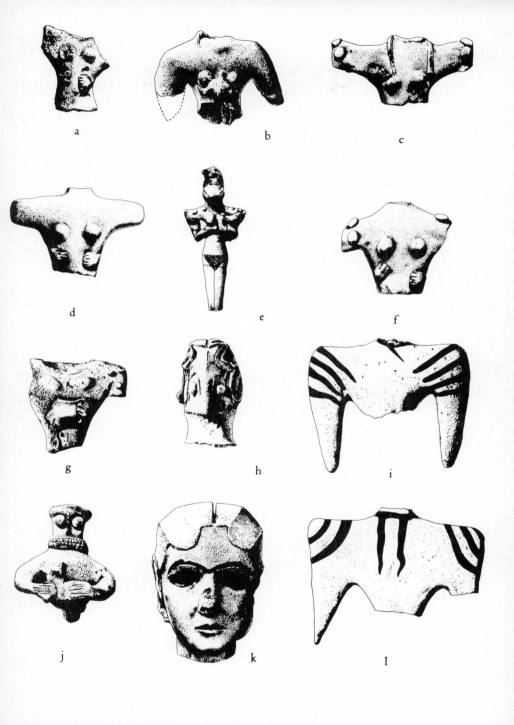

a

b

c

d

e

f

g

h

i

j

k

l

modified when they came in contact with local south Turkmenian traditions of figurine manufacture.

The above-mentioned parallels apply mainly to southern Mesopotamia, but fresh evidence obtained recently has expanded the area of cultural contacts as far as the basin of the River Diyala. In this respect the diffusion in Mesopotamia during the third millennium BC of clay figurines of men holding animals in their hands is very significant. A very similar figurine to these (but female) was found in Geoksyur I, which again indicates the existence of Mesopotamian influence on south Turkmenian figurines. This iconographic influence, however, was modified to suit local predilections by making the image female instead of male.

Still more significant in this respect is the clay head from the Namazga III period, found at Ulug-depe. This has the usual 'bird-like' face with incised almond-shaped eyes and applied pupils. The coiffure, however, received very elaborate treatment and contrasts sharply with the carelessly modelled face. The hair is parted from the forehead into two strands and the face is flanked by two rows of locks. This coiffure, unique among *Fig. 23k* south Turkmenian figurines, has close affinities with that of the beautiful marble head from the E-anna shrine at Uruk and, to a still greater extent, with that of the clay head from Choga Mami in the basin of the River Diyala. It has been widely assumed that the marble head from Uruk is the product of a purely Mesopotamian art school with its origin in the faces portrayed on the painted ware of Samarra. All this indicates the existence of definite cultural connections between Mesopotamia and southern Turkmenia and the impact of Mesopotamian culture on the culture of southern Turkmenia.

In this respect the Ubaidian influence is significant, making its appearance during the Namazga III period in the form of 'seal-amulets', which had been entirely unknown among the southern Turkmenian tribes until this period. These amulets were modified to the extent that their decoration copied exactly the geometric motifs of the native painted ware.

The same applies to long pins which were very common in the Namazga III period. These were straight, or twisted, thickened at one end and flattened at the other. Such objects were entirely unknown in the preceding period, but are frequently found in the graves of the Namazga III period. It is interesting to note that copper pins of this type have been found in Mesopotamia and Iran. One found at Geoksyur has two flat ends and looks like those from Mesopotamia in the Ubaid period.

All this points to increasing cultural contacts of southern Turkmenia with the western areas of Asia. It is highly probable however, that the predominance of analogies with Mesopotamia, and not with neigh-bouring Iran, may be explained by the fact that the northern parts of Iran have not yet been studied sufficiently well. It is hardly likely that the above-mentioned connections between Mesopotamia and south-western Central Asia could by-pass the territory of Iran in between.

These observable Irano-Mesopotamian cultural influences should not be allowed to overshadow the basic local line of evolution of the southern Turkmenian tribes. Even in the case of the Geoksyur Oasis we have no reason to assume that the local population was wholly replaced by newcomers. The continued existence here of only two villages —Geoksyur I and Chong-depe—is to be explained not so much by external influences as by their internal context, no small part in which was played by the natural changes in ancient hydrography.

It has been established by palaeogeographical research that at the turn of the fourth millennium BC the old delta channels of the River Tedjen, where the Geoksyur Oasis once stood, was suffering from excessive silt-ing. As a result, the permanent watercourse gave way to erratic streams. This must have caused the local population to build special reservoirs near the villages. Indeed one such reservoir, about 40 m. in diameter and over 3 m. deep, has been uncovered near the village of Mullali-depe, and was apparently connected with one of the delta channels, which served to replenish its water supply during rainy seasons. Excavations produced some sherds of the Geoksyur type of pottery from its silt deposits, but did not penetrate to the bottom of the reservoir where material of the Yalangach period might have been found. Still greater hydrographical changes in the Geoksyur Oasis must have taken place throughout the first half of the third millennium BC, which may be accounted for primarily by the westward shifting of the old delta. On this account a whole irrigation system was built near Geoksyur I, as has been established by aerial photography.

Fig. 24

In the silt deposits of one of the canals, where it joins with an old stream, a typical Geoksyurian female figurine of clay was found. It is quite possible that the ancient dwellers of Geoksyur I cast their deities into the water in the hope of getting better crops; unless this female figurine got here by accident, we have evidence of a close association of figurines with the idea of fertility coming from water.

In the middle of the third millennium BC the shifting of the Tedjen delta caused the local people to abandon the Geoksyur Oasis and move elsewhere. It is believed that most of them migrated to the middle reaches of this river and set up the village of Khapuz-depe, for the lower occupation levels of this village contain material which obviously continues the late Geoksyur traditions.

At the same time it is quite possible that a group of people migrated still further south, as far as what is now the territory of Afghanistan and Baluchistan. It is interesting to note, in this period, the development of the so-called Quetta culture in the south of Afghanistan (Mundigak) and in the north of Baluchistan.

THE QUETTA CULTURE

There are very many hypotheses regarding the origin of the Quetta culture. Piggott, who was the first to define it as such, suggested that it had originated in the Buff Ware culture of south-western Iran, Fairservis, however, was inclined to think that the Quetta culture was basically of local origin, although he suggested the possibility of Irano-Turkmenian influences. In the opinion of Kasal, on the other hand, the Quetta culture influenced the formation of the Geoksyurian complex of southern Turkmenia. The geometric patterns, such as crosses, stepped pyramids, and serrated lines which appeared on the pottery of south-eastern Turkmenia at the turn of the fourth millennium BC are similar, and at times identical to those on the Quetta ware. These analogies are not limited to painted pottery, but are also found in the small anthropomorphic figurines, certain metal artifacts, stamp seals and finally in similar types of burials.

In addition we find collective burials in rectangular chambers, similar to those found in Geoksyur I, Altin-depe and Ulug-depe. It is worth noting that collective burials in *tholoi* in southern Turkmenia date back to the fourth-third millennia BC, which means they carry much older traditions than their equivalent in southern Afghanistan. In other words, there are clear-cut analogies in such conservative and lasting traditions as funeral rites, which can hardly be dismissed as accidental.

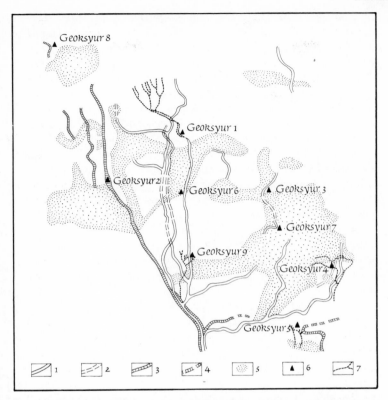

Fig. 24   Plan of the Geoksyur oasis, with Chalcolithic settlements and the hydrographic network, obtained from aerial photographs. 1 course of irrigation channel of the later fourth millennium BC; 2 its possible further course; 3 course of early third millennium BC channel; 4 possible course; 5 sand deposits; 6 settlements; 7 small channels from the final stages of irrigation

All this provides evidence to support the hypothesis that the Quettan complex was formed under the influence of south-east Turkmenian cultures. Although the Damb Sadaat II occupation was dated to 1850–2250 BC, and there was thus an apparent chronological gap between it and the time of the decline of the Geoksyur Oasis (in the middle of the third millennium BC), the new dating (2559± 202 BC) has narrowed this gap. It is important to note, however, that the Quettan pottery does not give the impression of having evolved directly from the Geoksyur-type pottery. As may be seen in the Quettan painted ware, the former Geoksyurian motifs and patterns seem to have been greatly modified. Before we can gauge with any certainty the extent of this influence on the Quettan culture, it is necessary to know what happened in the inter-mediate areas. We have assumed, however, that the process of infiltration of Central Asian tribes into Afghanistan and Baluchistan was slow and occurred mainly in the second half of the third millennium BC. As we shall show later in this account, the Mundigak IV assemblage has very convincing analogies especially in the culture of the south Turkmenian tribes in the Early Bronze (Namazga IV) period. There is no evidence, however, that the evolution from the Buff Ware culture into the Geoksyur is not connected with south-western Iran. After all, the origins of the Quetta-Geoksyur pottery are to be found in southern Iran. It is true, however, that the evolution from the Buff Ware culture into the Geoksyur culture, and later into the Quettan culture, has not yet been traced satisfactorily since some important intermediate links are still missing, and since the Quetta culture itself cannot be directly associated with the Suza pottery. On the whole, it seems that the Quettan culture is the result of the evolution of local clans which undoubtedly were open to the influence of neighbouring tribes, including those of southern Turkmenia.

CONCLUSION

To conclude this survey of the culture of the southern Turkmenian tribes of the Late Chalcolithic, it should be stressed that the local clans featured prominently on the historical scene of this period. It was then that large settlements with a complicated social organization were formed, though lack of written records makes it difficult to make any more specific description of the social structure of the period. But the construction of an irrigation system and the presence of large family clans who lived in multi-roomed houses clearly show that all forms of social life had become much more developed and complicated than before.

The extensive cultural connections with the neighbouring tribes, which at times took the form of migrations, clearly indicate that southern Turkmenia was the northern outpost of the ancient Near East.

CHAPTER VII

The Early Bronze Age
2500–2000 BC

The second half of the third millennium BC was marked by the advent of a new epoch—the Early Bronze Age. For lack of sufficient material, we cannot assert that it was exactly at this time that articles of bronze completely replaced those of copper. The term 'Early Bronze Age' refers to a new, more advanced stage of development observed at this time both in the material culture and in the economy as compared with the Chalcolithic Age that preceded it. Although we do not today have at our disposal all the information that might point to the advent of a new epoch, we do have definite evidence of qualitative changes which took place within the local society during the Early Bronze Age.

ECONOMIC DEVELOPMENT

From the middle of the third millennium BC there arose two kinds of settlement in southern Turkmenia: the larger, proto-urban settlements and much smaller village settlements. Parallel with this process can be observed changes in the economy, connected with the development of pottery manufacture. This is the period when the primitive pottery kiln of the Chalcolithic Age was universally replaced by firing furnaces. Approximately at this time also, another important device came into general use—the potter's wheel that eventually entirely replaced hand modelling. Without a doubt these two developments point to the isolation of a caste of professional potters from among the local farming and stock-breeding communities.

The use of relatively sophisticated drilling tools in the manufacture of various stone artifacts, particularly stone vessels, shows that there was also specialization in this ancient craft. The discovery of copper-smelting furnaces, too, indicates something more than merely the continued development of metal working; while the appearance of the first stone and ceramic seals marks a significant advance and, finally, the monumental structures that have been preserved can leave no doubt as to the complex transformations that occurred among the local tribes in the second half of the third millennium BC.

As in the preceding period, southern Turkmenia in the Early Bronze Age remained the most highly developed area in Western Central Asia, and general progress among the local tribes was such that they attained a level of culture in certain respects approaching that of the early urban society of the Ancient Near East.

NAMAZGA IV

In archaeological terms, the Early Bronze Age occurs in the period of Namazga IV, which in turn coincides with the early phase of Anau III. The corresponding occupation levels of this time at various settlements reach a thickness of 4–9 m., with the most characteristic feature of the assemblage comprising the painted ware, which had disappeared entirely by the beginning of the second millennium BC.

Two main types of settlement characterize this period: the village settlement of up to 2½ acres in area, sometimes a good deal less (Ak-depe, Anau, Shor-depe, Kosha-depe), and the proto-urban settlement, whose area extended to 60 or more acres (Namazga-depe, Ulug-depe, Khapuz-depe, Altin-depe). Recent research has shown that a number of the village settlements were rebuilt in the later stages of the Namazga IV period. In this connection the appearance of an entirely new oasis of village settlements in the vicinity of Artyk-Baba Durmaz (Taichanak-depe, Shor-depe, Kosha-depe) is significant. All these villages contain in their lowest occupation levels, which are stratified immediately above the bedrock, material of the late Namazga IV period. Since the material of the basal levels of these villages represents the purely local assemblage of Namazga IV type, we may safely assume that here was a case of local tribes resettling on account of the sharp rise in the population of large settlements. Thus, the formation of a new oasis in the vicinity of Artyk-Baba Durmaz is most probably the result of people being ousted from the nearby large settlement of Namazga-depe, where the agricultural economy could by this time apparently no longer satisfy the needs of a greatly increased population. These people were constrained to build their villages on the banks of shallow mountain streams flowing down from the foot-hills of Kopet Dag.

Unfortunately, we know little as yet of the actual structure and layout of the villages of the Early Bronze Age; the results of some partial excavations have led to the suggestion that the large villages already had

Fig. 25

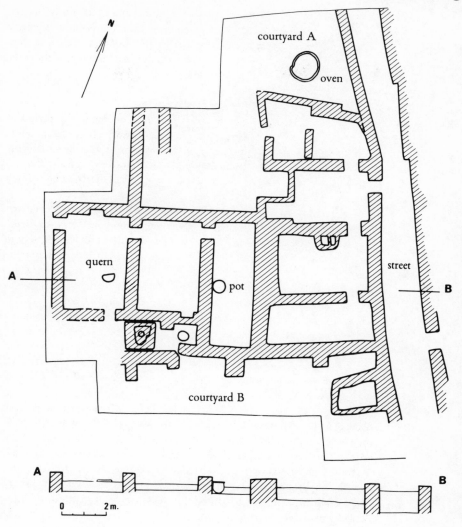

courtyard A

oven

N

quern

A

pot

street

B

courtyard B

A

B

0   2 m.

Fig. 25   Altin-depe; plan and section of the living quarters

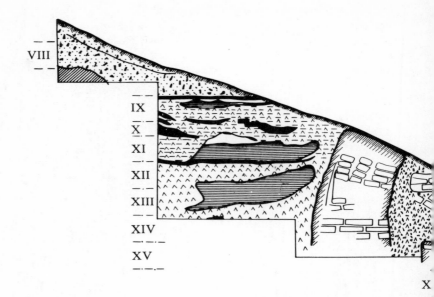

Fig. 26   Altin-depe; section through the fortification wall of the Namazga IV period

Fig. 26

defence walls; this hypothesis was mainly based on Altin-depe, where a massive wall 60 m. long, 2 m. thick and about 5 m. high was uncovered on the north-eastern edge of the settlement. The outside surface was buttressed by projecting pilasters measuring 0.5 sq. m. It has been established that the erection of this wall dates back to the earliest phase of the Namazga IV period, although it was later reconstructed. On the other hand, a whole series of trenches excavated at other places around the edge of that same settlement failed to uncover any trace of such a wall. Furthermore it turned out that the northern boundary of Altin-depe coincided with a wall no more than 0.5 m. thick, which belonged to an ordinary multi-roomed house. No defence walls dating to this time were found at Ulug-depe either.

At the present time therefore it seems very likely that the massive wall at Altin-depe is all that remains of some kind of monumental cult or administrative building. In short, there seems to be no definite evidence of special defence walls even in large settlements of the Early Bronze Age.

The available information about the type of structures used in private dwellings is also very limited. This unfortunate gap has been filled to a certain extent by finds made during the excavations at Khapuz-depe,

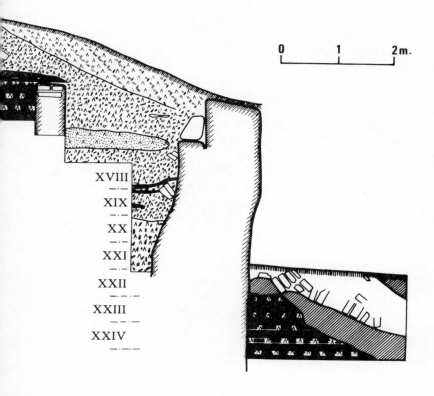

the settlement to the south of the Geoksyur Oasis. A small excavation of some 150 sq. m. exposed ten interconnecting rooms in Early Bronze Age occupation levels, forming a part of a single compact dwelling complex. These are spacious rooms with round hearths dug into the floor that have been described as living areas, and small kitchens with similar hearths set in one corner. The excavated complex includes a rectangular room with two clay 'podiums' placed in the centre of the wall facing each other; such rooms may have been small domestic shrines. There is no doubt, however, that the excavated section belonged to a multi-roomed house very similar to those of the Late Chalcolithic period.

The same basic type of building was found during excavations at Ulug-depe, where one trench uncovered three successive building levels of this period. A straight street was flanked on either side by two isolated dwelling complexes, consisting of living and domestic rooms. It is interesting to note that the general direction of the street and the basic distribution of the interconnecting rooms were retained in two building levels.

A similar type of building in a small settlement came to light at Ak-depe near Ashkhabad. Here, in the upper building level, twelve rooms were excavated, which judging from the objects found in them, comprised living and domestic rooms and possibly a shrine. The floors and walls in a number of the rooms were found to have been faced with alabaster. Among the domestic rooms were storerooms containing large vessels. The multi-roomed type of house seems, therefore, to have been common to all the settlements, although our information is far from complete.

Fig. 27

In the Early Bronze Age, the two pottery styles of the preceding period were replaced by a unified painted pottery style. That of the Namazga IV culture occurs in the eastern and central zones, taking into account of course, local variations. The painted pottery of this period is chiefly monochrome, decorated with small patterns forming friezes; these were mostly geometric patterns, the old zoomorphic motifs having practically disappeared. On isolated vessels schematic bird motifs occur, or more realistically portrayed goat figures, often standing between two trees and, significantly, represented in a style entirely different from that of the Late Chalcolithic period. This association of trees and caprids calls to

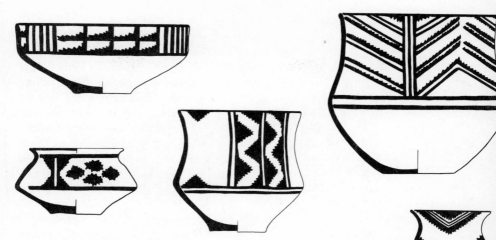

Fig. 27   Pottery of Namazga IV type

mind the theme of goats guarding the tree of life which was extremely popular in the ancient Near East, a motif which very possibly found its way from there to the settlements of southern Turkmenia.

In general, three categories of pottery may be distinguished in this period: painted, unpainted and grey. As we shall show later, the grey ware was more common in the western districts which were populated by local tribes.

To date, the most complete stratified sequence of habitation levels providing a picture of the local development of pottery from the Late Chalcolithic Age to the Early Bronze Age, has been obtained from excavations at Khapuz-depe.

Immediately above the alluvial bedrock a culture layer one metre thick was found to contain painted pottery very close in style to that of the latest settlements of the Geoksyur Oasis, the decoration consisting of large patterns on a bright red slipped ground. This has led to the supposition that Khapuz-depe was founded by settlers from the Geoksyur Oasis after human occupation there had finally ceased in the third millennium BC. Broadly speaking, this lowest layer represents an intermediate phase between the Late Chalolithic culture (Namazga III) and the Early Bronze Age culture (Namazga IV). The 5 m.-thick stratum above it contained painted pottery typical of the latter.

The decoration of the painted pottery at Khapuz-depe is basically geometric, but the patterns become so minute that the friezes seem confused and crowded with detailed elements. In addition, there now appear sporadic new motifs—stepped and unstepped pyramids, mostly small in size, all of which originated in the post-Geoksyurian style.

The shapes of the vessels themselves, comprising, for the most part, goblets with straight vertical sides and a sharply sloping base, as well as hemispherical bowls and cups and conical cups, can all be traced back to the preceding period although there are also novelties such as sharply ribbed vessels. This latter feature resulted directly from the use of the potter's wheel which facilitated the manufacture of more fanciful forms.

The predominant use of a red ground, and the retention, though with certain modifications, of the geometric motifs of the post-Geoksyurian style, including polychrome decoration, leaves no doubt as to the genetic connection between the Namazga IV complex and the Late Chalcolithic pottery that preceded it in south-western Turkmenia. The ceramic sequence observed at Khapuz-depe becomes even more significant when we realize that the pottery of even the earliest phase of the Namazga IV complex was manufactured on the potter's wheel. Some large vessels recovered from the lower layers of the settlement have the main body made entirely by hand while the flaring rim bears the marks of the regular concentric circles that we associate with wheel-turned pottery. And yet, judging by the ceramic sequence at Khapuz-depe, the potter's wheel was only introduced gradually.

Throughout the entire 5 m. depth of the Namazga IV culture layer hand-shaped vessels occur alongside those bearing the unmistakable stamp of the potter's wheel. This enables us to date the introduction of the potter's wheel into southern Turkmenia to the middle, rather than the end, of the third millennium BC.

In general, we find a similar development in pottery manufacture in the other large settlement of the Early Bronze Age in south-western Turkmenia: Altin-depe. Although excavations here were limited in scale, the pottery was found to correspond fairly closely to that of Khapuz-depe; having black and brown painted designs on a red or cream-coloured ground. Nearly all the painted pottery from Altin-depe at this time was wheel-turned; the clay is of good quality, without admixture of vegetable matter, the firing excellent. The decoration follows the general

Plate 32

pattern of Khapuz-depe, with, however, finer workmanship in many cases. This is perhaps to be explained by the fact that Altin-depe was one of the more centrally located settlements, as compared with Khapuz-depe, which was even then a remote outpost on the periphery of the agricultural world of that time.

The pottery from the settlement of Ulug-depe dating to the Namazga IV period is of great interest; both in the shape of the vessels and the type of decoration it resembles the pottery at Altin-depe, except that pots with a light-coloured slip are to be found alongside pottery with a red ground. Thus there seem to be two ceramic traditions having their origins in the older techniques of the eastward and central zones of southern Turkmenia respectively.

Plates 33, 34

Alongside the preponderating geometric patterns, there were isolated cases of designs featuring goats and birds. That pottery from the Central Zone was also imported in large quantities is easy to understand when it is remembered that Ulug-depe stood on the border between these two regions. The presence of a 'double' pottery vessel with painted decoration in the Ulug-depe grave is significant since it is the only instance of such a shape being found in southern Turkmenia.

The pottery of this period in Namazga-depe and Anau is distinguished by a high standard of workmanship and rather fanciful forms. Characteristic too is the frequent use of ribbing as decoration; in this connection, the pottery of the central region is closer to the contemporary pottery of Ulug-depe and Altin-depe than to that of Khapuz-depe. Minor peculiarities of the pottery of this region merely reflect the variations in techniques used by local potters.

Unfortunately, the available evidence of Early Bronze Age pottery in the western region is even less informative. It is interesting to note, for example at the settlement of Ak-depe near Ashkhabad, that alongside the ordinary painted pottery, typical of Namazga IV, there was a large amount of grey, partially burnished pottery with incised decoration. Besides these grey pots there were sharply ribbed goblets of bizarre shape standing on crimped, often hollow, pedestals. Worthy of note, too, is the scratched decoration in patterns comprising groups of vertical stripes of horizontal wavy lines. A characteristic method of decoration used little coiled snakes applied to the wall of the vessel, resulting in an elegant design of great expressiveness. It should be noted that similar

Fig. 28

examples of grey pottery with incised decoration have been found in contemporary culture layers in practically every settlement in southern Turkmenia, but the percentage of such vessels in these other areas is negligible compared with the painted pottery, and would indicate that the grey pottery was imported from the more western settlements, such as Ak-depe.

The great frequency of grey pottery in Ak-depe and certain other settlements in south-western Turkmenia shows the extent of the influence northern Iran extended on southern Turkmenia. This ties in with the fact that the settlements of the western region are territorially the closest to such Iranian settlements as Tyureng-tepe and Shakh-tepe, where grey clay pottery was very common in the mid third millennium BC. There is no reason to believe that the grey pottery came to northern Iran from Western Central Asia, as certain authorities have stated. It is interesting to note that in the burial chambers of Altin-depe, one assemblage contains both painted vessels with large patterns and plain ware which was more characteristic of the pottery of the subsequent Middle Bronze Age (Namazga V).

Great progress in the techniques of pottery production was achieved by a new type of kiln which became a feature of the early period of the Bronze Age, as attested, for example, by excavations at Namazga-depe and Khapuz-depe. The rather primitive one-tier kilns of the previous period were replaced by much larger kilns of a more complicated design. These have two tiers, the firing chamber being built over the brick-lined furnace. A vertical partition or a thick pillar was built into the centre of the furnace to support the firing chamber above it, while the horizontal partition dividing the two chambers was perforated in many places to convey the heat. The furnace was loaded with firewood through a special wide opening so that the heated air was drawn into the chamber. It is interesting to note that the firing chamber was constructed with a domed covering made of bricks with a special hatch through which the leather-hard pottery was passed into the kiln.

The operation of these two-tiered kilns, where considerations of temperature adjustment and timing were of great importance, obviously required great technological skill. The use of the potter's wheel and kilns of complicated design leaves no doubt as to the existence of professional potters at that time.

Fig. 28   Grey pottery from Ak-depe. 1 : 6

The employment of advanced techniques is also indicated by the discovery of two copper smelting furnaces on the outskirts of Khapuz-depe. Here both copper slag and broken clay ladles, still retaining traces of molten copper, were found. The fact that the slag waste was still rich in metal points to a poor standard of smelting without any knowledge of the forced draught, while it has been established that these furnaces were used repeatedly. The presence of iron in the slag indicates the existence of a common source of both metals used at this site.

In the Namazga IV occupation levels both single and larger collective burials in rectangular chambers were excavated. Collective burials, however, are more common in south-eastern Turkmenia, which again points to the continuity of the local post-Geoksyur traditions; they have been found at Khapuz-depe and Altin-depe but are still unknown in the central area, for example, at Namazga-depe.

The available evidence suggests that collective burials in separate chambers belonged more to the early phase of the Namazga IV period. In the later phase, specially constructed burial chambers were gradually replaced by collective burials in abandoned dwelling complexes which were divided by thin partitions into several chambers for this purpose. Funeral offerings were rather poor, but the number of pottery vessels in graves was greater than in the preceding period. One of the most characteristic articles found in graves were oil lamps (sconces) carved out of a marble-like stone. Most of these lamps are cylindrical with a tapering base; the upper part has a shallow depression covered by a lid with a hole in the centre. One lamp was found with a wick still preserved in the cover. The discovery of such lamps in graves indicates that burial rites

had become more complex and that in this period the after-world was imagined as a dark and gloomy place.

Although in the Early Bronze Age there were fewer anthropomorphic figurines than in the preceding period, it has been possible to identify several iconographic types. Most of them are female figurines without arms and breasts, and all are seated. Baked clay and stone figurines of this type, true to the iconographic traditions of the late Geoksyur period, were found at Khapuz-depe. The same continuity of the south Turkmenian figurine style is reflected in the seated figurines with exaggerated female sexual attributes. In general, painted decoration of statuettes, which was typical of the Chalcolithic period, was superseded in the Early Bronze Age by incised and excised patterns. An increasing number of figurines had coiffures in the form of two straight plaits falling on the breast and a third plait down the back. This stylistic innovation had first appeared in the Late Chalcolithic period, but was fully developed in the statuary of the Bronze Age.

Along with this purely local development in the clay figurine tradition, some figurines were executed in a highly individual style. For example, one statuette found in Altin-depe shows a pregnant woman with her protruding stomach covered in small pin pricks. This rare figurine presents a new iconographic image possibly symbolizing the idea of conception and motherhood. Another figurine from Altin-depe had been given a coiffure of short plaits flanking her face. This type of coiffure is entirely unknown in other figurines from south Turkmenia, but is characteristic of the anthropomorphic figurines of Tell Tainat in Syria.

Two other rare figurines were recovered from Namazga-depe and Altin-depe respectively; both had one arm held straight against the body and the other bent at the elbow with the hand touching the face. Some female and male figurines had cylindrical bases, the closest analogies of which are the statuettes of the Zkhob type in Pakistan. Yet in all other respects (near-square shoulders, plaits hanging down the chest, numerous applied clay bosses and strips) these figurines were clearly developed from local figurines of the Late Chalcolithic period.

Found in conjunction with these standard figurines mass-produced for everyday use, were also much more sophisticated monumental examples which were probably not images of the god for individual private contemplation, but objects of public worship. The torso of one such statue, carved out of white marble, was found at Namazga-depe. The upper part of the torso is hollowed out to receive a tenon connecting it to the separately carved head which, unfortunately, was never found.

Although it is still difficult to trace the main line of evolution of anthropomorphic figurines during the second half of the third millennium BC, it is quite possible that the late phase of Namazga IV saw the emergence of an iconographic type which was to become very popular in the subsequent Middle Bronze Age. A female figurine found at Altin-depe is important in this respect: a flat statuette (unlike the traditionally three-dimensional figurines) seated, with outspread arms, it is an entirely new iconographic type, although evolved from the local anthropomorphic statuary.

On the whole the Early Bronze Age is a period of experiment and creative innovation in the field of sculpture, which produced a new type of female deity, and implies profound changes in religious ideas in this period. This is also reflected in the male figurines with highly schematic faces, but with exaggerated phalluses. Finally, there is an isolated group of sporadic miniature figurines with outspread and sometimes slightly bent legs without any indication of sex. Some of them have deep pin-prick markings on the back and the stomach, the significance of which is not apparent.

Although on the whole the anthropomorphic figurines have a distinctly uniform style which is characteristic of all southern Turkmenia, the female figurines from Ak-depe near Ashkhabad are distinguished to a certain extent from the others mainly in their standing position and grey colour. In this respect they resemble the figurines from Tyureng-tepe.

Most of the zoomorphic figurines, predominantly camels, are represented in the same conventionalized style. But of exceptional historic and economic significance is the fact that many of these camels are attached by their long necks to miniature baked clay carts. This is important evidence that camels in this period were used as draught animals.

Plate 36

The Namazga IV period also saw the gradual displacement of amulets by seals, some of the earliest of which were found at Ulug-depe. These were flat square stones with two perforations in the centre for suspension by a cord and with a pattern on one side. The geometric patterns, and particularly those made by drilling small holes along the contours of the design, have their closest analogies in the seals found at Mundigak and other sites in Afghanistan. So similar are they, that we must conclude that these two groups of finds are in some way connected. It is still difficult to establish whether these seals spread from southern Afghanistan to southern Turkmenia or *vice versa*, while an independent diffusion to these countries is also a possibility.[1]

Although these stone artifacts reflect an early stage in the development of seals, their loop-handles leave no doubt as to their function. The discovery of a ceramic seal in the same occupation level as the stone seals at Ulug-depe provides additional evidence of their development. This clay seal is heavy and square with an excised pattern of little crosses on one surface, and a loop-handle on the other. The excised decoration imitates known patterns on south Turkmenian painted ware, which clearly shows that the seals were made locally.

The appearance of seals in this period signifies important changes within the society of the Early Bronze Age. This period was also marked by the development of stone carving, as seen in the skilfully chiselled beads and pendants. A new element was introduced by the production of large biconical ornaments made of pieces of different coloured stones. The extensive use of a primitive drilling device is confirmed by the discovery of stone vessels of symmetrical shape. These are mostly small cylindrical containers narrowing towards the top with the upper edge curving slightly outwards.

Plate 35

Flint was still widely used in the manufacture of arrow-heads, as seen for example in the material from Khapuz-depe. These are of two types—large leaf-shaped arrow-heads with bifacial retouch, and a smaller variety retouched at the tip with three-faceted tangs. Since Khapuz-depe is situated at a great distance from the mountains, it seems likely that the arrow-heads got here as a result of trade exchange or that the inhabitants of Khapuz-depe sent expeditions to the mountains for this commodity. It is quite possible that the inhabitants of the Geoksyur Oasis in previous periods did exactly the same thing.

The presence of flint arrow-heads in such numbers—50 at Khapuz-depe alone—indicates the rather limited use of metal in this period. Although the traces of two foundries have been excavated at Khapuz-depe, the copper objects found lack variety. They include needles with eyes, piercers, awls, long pins with flattened heads, and miniature pins with bipyramidal heads. The excavations also revealed pins with heads in the form of a stepped pyramid or a cruciform terminal. It is clear that all these decorations are exact copies of the patterns on painted pottery, which shows that local motifs were used in metalwork.

CONCLUSION

On the whole the Early Bronze Age is distinguished by cultural unification throughout the entire territory of southern Turkmenia which, of course, does not exclude the possibility of local variants. One such local variant, which was probably formed as a result of territorial proximity to north-western Iran, seems to be associated with the western part of the country, having been found at Ak-depe, near Ashkhabad. The eastern parts of Turkmenia, on the other hand, were drawn more and more into the sphere of influence of Pakistan and Baluchistan.

Notwithstanding the cultural unification, profound changes undoubtedly occurred in the local society of the Early Bronze Age, in association with technological developments; the formation of two types of settlements, including the proto-urban variety consisting of multi-roomed houses which formed whole residential areas, the use of seals, the appearance of monumental architecture, and the gradual evolution of one common iconographic image of a female deity, all testify to the qualitative changes that found their full expression in the Middle Bronze Age.

CHAPTER VIII

Urban Civilization in Turkmenia

2000–1600 BC

The economic and social phenomena described in the previous chapter led to important changes in community living in southern Turkmenia in the Early Bronze Age and the appearance of proto-urban civilization. Gordon Childe aptly called this process the 'urban revolution', meaning by this the qualitative changes that affected the life of society. It would seem, however, that although Childe's concept was fundamentally correct, it needs clarification. For example, this outstanding prehistorian considered the class structure of society as one of the characteristic features of the urban revolution. In our view the very emergence of this structure, which divides prehistoric classless society from class society is the direct result of the urban revolution which primarily affected the economic basis of society. The urban revolution should be regarded as the establishment of the economic basis of early class society, which process manifested itself in the ancient Near East in the appearance of urban civilizations.

In the material of the Old World we can isolate two models of this process, the first model being the Sumerian. Here the urban revolution took place in a highly productive agricultural economy based on irrigation in fertile, subtropical valleys. Under these conditions, urban civilizations developed, as a rule, independently of each other and at a relatively early period (Sumer, Elam, Egypt, Harappa and the late Shang period of China).[1] Most of the achievements in these regions, including the technique of writing, were of local origin.

The second, or Anatolian model is characteristic of a society which either used irrigation-agriculture on a very limited scale, or did not use it at all. The smaller increase in the public surplus product retarded the rate of social development, and urban civilization arose here much later, employing existing cultural forms, including a written language, which had already been developed in some other area where the urban revolution had taken place much earlier. This process of development is typical of northern Mesopotamia, Syria, Palestine, and Asia Minor. Judging by the available information, this was the pattern followed by the agriculturists of southern Turkmenia. The related processes in this region were most clearly manifest during the Middle Bronze Age, or the Namazga V period, (according to the stratigraphical sequence worked out by Kuftin for Namazga-depe).

The Namazga V complex is characterized by plain pottery, mostly with a light-coloured slip. Its emergence coincides with the disappearance of painted pottery of the Namazga IV type, its end coincides with the period when grey- and red-slipped pottery came into fashion, as part of the Namazga VI assemblage. The analogies with Mesopotamia, Iran (the Hissar III complex) and Harappa of both the Middle and, to a lesser extent, the Late Bronze Age, have made it possible tentatively to date the Namazga V complex to the mid-second millennium BC possibly beginning as early as the third millennium BC. The latest building level of Namazga IV type at Altin-depe has been dated by Carbon 14 to 2120 ($\pm$ 50) BC.

Thus in southern Turkmenia the urban revolution continued for about four to five centuries. The first indication of these great changes is the formation and development of large villages with specific areas for craftsmen and traders, which was a characteristic feature of the entire period. In southern Turkmenia the origins of this process go back at least to the Early Bronze Age.

During the Namazga V period the most important centre in southern Turkmenia was, of course, Namazga-depe. Its sprawling ruins cover about 170 acres and comprise a large number of habitation layers with a total thickness of up to 34 m. However, Namazga-depe is notable not only for its size, but for its material culture; the pottery in particular, has an elegance which testifies to high technological skill. At Namazga-depe, large sections of a built-up area have been excavated. Most of the structures, separated from each other by narrow streets, were multi-roomed dwelling-complexes with open-courtyards next to them. That life here was not devoid of comforts is shown by a ceramic trough, all that remains of what was probably an ancient water supply system. The dwelling complexes consisted of 9–12 rooms and sometimes even more. Niches for pottery were built into the walls and sometimes also contained stoves for heating. Other buildings were essentially different from these, and may have served a religious purpose. One of these, occupying a

Plate 39

separate mound in the south-eastern section of the settlement, had walls made of clay blocks which were almost one metre thick: several narrow rooms opened into a large square courtyard. This building is probably the remains of a temple or shrine. Unfortunately, since most of the area of this site was occupied by a cemetery of a later period, extensive excavations and mapping of this ancient settlement were somewhat impeded, and are not, therefore, sufficiently accurate to allow more detailed conclusions about its planning.

The research carried out at Namazga-depe clearly shows that the village was not a mere agglomeration of dwellings, but an important production centre. Broken ladles and copper slag testify to the existence of developed metallurgy, and in some places traces of metal smelting furnaces have also been found. These were generally located in groups and no doubt constituted the workshops or artisans' quarters. In a house around one such group of pottery kilns a large box was found, filled with finished fired vessels. The two-tiered kilns themselves were of the same construction as in the preceding period. Namazga-depe in the Middle Bronze Age was clearly a large populated centre with developed crafts.

Plate 48

These characteristic features of an emergent town are even more apparent in Altin-depe. This second capital of southern Turkmenia is smaller than Namazga-depe, but has been studied in greater detail; its flooded ruins occupy an area of 114 acres. In the southern part of the site a wide sloping depression marks what was once the entrance to a large central square. In the northwest lay the residential area which made up the greater part of Altin-depe. A trial trench here revealed the traces of two dwelling complexes divided by either a courtyard or a street. At the very edge of the settlement stood a group of pottery kilns.

Most of the pottery was made on the so-called 'Craftsmen's mound', more than 6 acres in area, where potters evidently lived and worked for a long time. Rejected and broken pottery, ceramic waste and remnants of kilns have been found there in great quantity. Excavations over a small area on the northern slope of the mound revealed ten such kilns, most of which were of the same construction as those found at Namazga-depe. The kilns stood next to multi-roomed structures which presumably included both living rooms and workrooms. Thus, for example, at Site 1, three building levels were excavated (Altin-depe 1-3) corresponding to the Namazga V period. Each of the levels contained two-tiered kilns and also traces of multi-roomed houses. Near one of the kilns numerous unbaked pottery objects were found, including 35 clay oxen, 14 anthropomorphic figurines, and 8 wheels from toy carts. Even though the place where the artisans lived and worked occupied a large area, these professional craftsmen do not appear to have been wealthy people: the burials uncovered in all three layers of Site I contained almost no burial goods, except for occasional bead-amulets, and these were rare.

In contrast to this quarter, the eastern side of Altin-depe bore the marks of prosperity. Thus the houses excavated on the so-called 'Tower mound' contained a bronze zoomorphic seal and two hoards buried in the walls. These hoards included clay vessels both of local and imported origin, and artifacts of bone, faience and ivory. From the systematic excavations of wealthy houses carried out on the 'Mound of the wall', it was possible to distinguish streets dividing the settlement into rectangular quarters. The width of the main street was 2 m. and that of the side lanes 1.5 m.– 1.8 m. At the same time the planning of the village was not strictly geo-metrical: the width of the streets and the direction in which they run was determined by the situation of the adjoining structures. The well-preserved doorways made it possible to distinguish separate dwelling complexes, consisting of two living rooms, two to three auxiliary rooms with adjoining courtyards, and a kitchen. The total floor space of each complex, excluding the courtyard, was 40–50 sq. m. The general aspect of these houses, as well as the functions they performed, shows that they were occupied by individual self-supporting families. They were of high quality with walls which were well plastered, often with many coats of daub and sometimes coated with red paint as well. That the people who lived on the 'Mound of the wall' were well-to-do is attested not only by the large quantities of vessels found intact in the houses, but also by the rich furnishings of the graves. For example, the grave-goods of a collec-tive burial containing fourteen skeletons, possibly belonging to one clan, comprised twenty clay vessels, a stone vessel, a clay anthropomorphic figurine, rings, beads, an arrow-head and two bronze zoomorphic seals. Still more impressive is the burial tentatively known as the 'priestess's grave', which contained the skeleton of a woman lying on her left side clutching two female figurines in her heavily ringed hand. In the same grave were about 100 beads made of agate, carnelian, lapis lazuli with

Fig. 29

Plate 43

Plate 40

Plate 46

gold binding and paste set in gold, as well as a silver seal in the shape of a fantastic three-headed beast of prey.

The flourishing specialist crafts and the living quarters crowded with people enjoying varying degrees of prosperity are not the only character-istic features of the incipient urban community of Altin-depe. Monu-mental architecture, older than any other of its kind yet found on the territory of the Soviet Union, was recently excavated on an isolated mound on the eastern side of Altin-depe, *i.e.* in the 'wealthy part' of the settlement. As the houses here had been rebuilt and repaired several times, it was very difficult to reconstruct the order in which these changes had taken place. It would seem, however, that there were three main periods in the evolution of this newly discovered complex.

The mound, 21 m. wide and oriented north-south, was originally formed of ruined dwellings from the Namazga IV period, the subse-quent houses being constructed on top of the ruins. The mound was then faced on three sides with sun-baked brick and turned into a stepped structure, an obvious imitation of the Mesopotamian ziggurats. So far the traces of four steps have been uncovered in this early ziggurat, which reached a height of 6 m. The outer face of the second step or plat-form was decorated with pilasters which were triple-stepped in plan.

The second period in the evolution of the mound was evidently a time of prosperity, when a whole new complex of monumental structures was built around those of the first period. Still oriented north-south, this complex was 45 m. long, and in its southern part was a large tower, inside which traces of the earlier ziggurat were found. The foundation platform of this new ziggurat was 2 m. high; the second step was in-creased in height to 3.5 or 4 m., but its new outer face was still decorated with triple-stepped pilasters. Thus the ziggurat of the second period had a total height of 12 m. when newly constructed. By analogy with the Mesopotamian sites, it seems that the ziggurat of Altin-depe was topped by a small shrine. During this second period, a house called the 'En-circled house' adjoined the ziggurat on its southern side. This house stood on a platform 3 m. high which was also decorated with pilasters. The rooms on this platform have only been partially preserved and, judging by their size and planning, were used for food storage.

The third period was marked by the gradual decay of the whole com-plex, followed by its partial restoration. In this period a structure

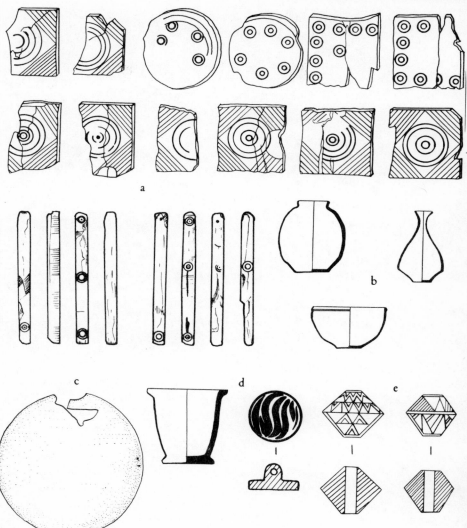

Fig. 29   Altin-depe; objects from the Namazga V period hoard. a bone; b pottery; c mirror; d faience; e stone

referred to as the 'Corner House' was built on to the south side of the ziggurat, thus increasing the width of the whole structure to 55 m. The weight of the brickwork without any terracing now caused the whole structure to tilt and parts of it to collapse; in order to check this process, special supports were built on the outer face of the wall, and the first step of the ziggurat itself was made thicker. Even so, the mass of brickwork continued to collapse, and ultimately the entire complex had to be abandoned. In the mass of debris at the outer edge of the platform supporting the 'Encircled House' a burial with pottery typical of the Namazga V period was excavated, enabling us to date the complex to some time during the Middle Bronze Age. Monumental structures are an important feature of the urban revolution, as was pointed out by Gordon Childe; they reflect the economic achievements of a society which could use its surplus commodities for purposes other than production. In general features the ziggurat at Altin-depe, despite the clumsy primitive design, follows Mesopotamian models and in this respect symbolizes the new epoch.[2]

Namazga-depe and Altin-depe were the principal cultural centres in the Bronze Age and were surrounded by a large number of smaller settlements. The largest of these was Ulug-depe near Dushak which occupied an area of about 25 acres.

The layers of the Namazga V period at Ulug-depe vary in depth from 2 to 3.5 m. On the south-western edge of the settlement was a cemetery containing the burials of a number of relatively wealthy people. One grave, for example, contained 27 pottery vessels, a stone censer and many paste beads. Another grave contained 23 vessels, a twisted bronze ring still on a finger and a large number of paste beads on the chest of the deceased; these may have been sewn on to the clothing. Other finds include a bronze pin with a spear-shaped head.

Plates 37, 38

While it has not yet been established if Ulug-depe had any monu-mental structures, it is evident that there were none in the small rural villages, for the total area occupied by these settlements was hardly larger than the monumental complex of Altin-depe alone. Such villages include the southern mound of Anau, Shor-depe near Baba-Durmaz station, Taichanak-depe west of Artyk station, and Khapuz-depe in the ancient delta of the River Tedjen. At Shor-depe fragments of several multi-roomed houses, crowded around small inner courtyards were excavated. It is significant that in this small village (its area is less than 5 acres) a zoomorphic bronze seal was found. Excavations show that a relatively high cultural level was also reached at Taichanak-depe. The excellent wheel-made pottery, a silver seal, and elegant female figurines found here are similar to those found at Altin-depe and Namazga-depe.

The very presence in this area of large proto-urban centres such as Namazga-depe and Altin-depe testifies to considerable economic prosperity, for only high agricultural productivity could have enabled a society to develop specialized crafts and, above all, to build large monu-mental structures. It is significant in this respect that the erection of the Altin-depe ziggurat alone required about half a million sun-dried bricks; the production of this number of bricks, coupled with the time taken to build the ziggurat, must have entailed a large labour force.

Unfortunately we know almost nothing about the agriculture of the Middle Bronze Age, though this undoubtedly was the economic basis of society in this period. At any rate the concentration in one place of large populations which lived in proto-urban centres would have been possible only with a stable system of cultivation. The Middle Bronze Age population very likely irrigated their fields artificially by taking water from small streams that ran down the Kopet Dag mountains. The irrigation techniques used at that time were no doubt relatively advanced, for the farmers most likely drew on the experience of the settlers of the Geoksyur Oasis in building irrigation works. The discovery of carbon-ized remains of trees such as ash, poplar and karagach shows that the water discharge of the streams and rivers in this period was higher than it is today, although the natural water supply in the submontane zone will have ruled out the possibility of complicated irrigation systems like those in Sumer or Elan. It was probably this particular factor which retarded the general cultural development in southern Turkmenia, for even in the period of Neolithic revolution the settlements here were considerably behind their contemporaries of the Near East.

The crops cultivated in the Middle Bronze Age were more varied than in the preceding Chalcolithic period: grains of wheat, barley, chick-pea and small grapes have been excavated. It is possible that a wooden plough was used for tilling the soil, and there is abundant evidence that draught cattle were used: clay models of four-wheeled carts with the heads of harnessed animals attached to the beam, for instance, have been found. Though these mostly took the form of camels, representations of horses also occur. Stockbreeding was mostly limited to the smaller varieties of animals such as goats and sheep. By way of example the late Namazga IV layers at Shor-depe contained the bones of 16 animals, only two of which were cows, while the Namazga V layers contained the bones of 10 animals all of which were sheep or goats. These were apparently pastured several days' journey away from the settlements, a practice followed in this region to this day.

Crafts, particularly pottery, reached the peak of their development in the Middle Bronze Age. In the Namazga V period almost all the pottery was made on a fast potter's wheel; it was fired in two-tiered kilns at a temperature of up to 1400° C, and the improved techniques led to considerable modifications in the appearance of the pottery. The smooth curved lines of the hand-made ware were replaced by intricate, deeply indented forms. At the same time the carelessly painted patterns which were typical of the late Namazga IV were almost entirely replaced by well-defined decorative designs. This feature is characteristic of pottery which was produced in quantity. Production of pottery, no doubt by skilled professional craftsmen, was strictly standardized, and there was a sharp increase in the variety of forms which, in the Namazga V period, comprised about 30 basic pottery types. The most characteristic are the pedestalled vases, biconical vessels, and vessels with spouts.[3] Pots joined by connecting mouths were a new development. Other objects included annular pot-stands, and hand-made globular, lipped vessels and flat braziers, which also became popular in the late Namazga V period. It is interesting to note that in the Middle Bronze Age in southern Turkmenia, hardly any of the pots had handles, in sharp contrast to the pottery of Iran and Mesopotamia.

Figs 30, 31   Metallurgy was also highly developed in this period, lead and arsenic often being added to the bronze. Some of the objects from Namazga-depe contained as much as 8–10 lead and in one case the artifact was even made of brass (an alloy of copper and zinc). Twin moulds were used for casting; precious metals including gold and silver were also used Hoards containing metal artifacts which may have belonged to pro-

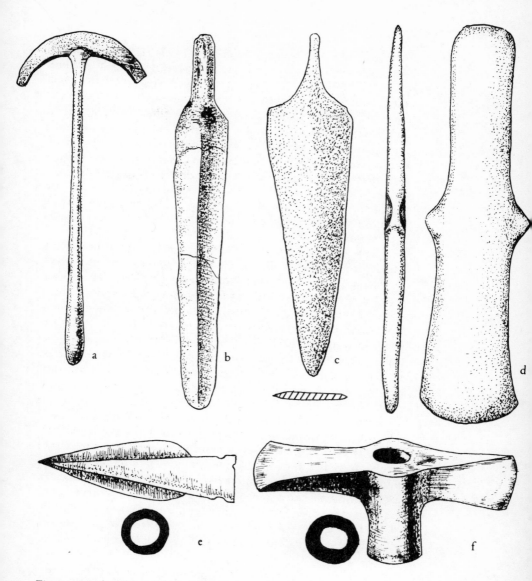

Fig. 30 Metal artifacts of the Bronze Age from southern Turkmenia. a, c, d Altin-depe; b Anau; e Ashkhabad; f Daina

fessional smiths or traders occur sporadically. One such hoard, found at Namazga-depe, contained a gouge, spears, so-called razors, mirrors and a ring.

Fig. 30

The artifacts manufactured in this period were such as are commonly associated with the Middle Bronze Age. Weapons and implements included types which were already widespread in southern Turkmenia: square cross-section awls, adzes, knives, leaf-shaped tanged spear-heads and the very typical flat-bladed knives and daggers without a midrib; spear-heads and daggers increased in number. A silver adze with trunnions found at Altin-depe was of quite a new type, as was the axe-adze from Daina in the north-western Kopet Dag mountains. Knives made of a special shape (the so-called 'razors') were probably used for chopping meat.

Fig. 31

A large variety of jewellery and toilet articles was manufactured. Rings (frequently of gold), round, slightly concave mirrors without handles, and temporal pendants were made as in the Chalcolithic period, as well as bracelets, some of which had several coils. Pins with a variety of carved heads were also common, and the fact that most of these were blunt-ended suggests that they were perhaps not used as pins, but were miniature models of staffs. The heads took the form of double spirals, sickles, spears, multi-stepped crosses, and even goats. The variety of these artifacts is not in itself a sign of increasingly complex social structure, but the proliferation of their decorative detail points to the rising pros-perity of their owners. The progress in metallurgy is illustrated by the appearance of bronze vessels—small pots and flat handled pans.

Plates 46, 47

Finally, large quantities of seals were produced and widely distributed. These were made of nearly every available material—stone, clay, and even turtle shells. Bronze and silver seals with a lug on the reverse side for suspension seem to have been the most popular. These, in particular, have been most frequently found in the ancient burials, always located near the pelvic bones, which may indicate that they were worn on a belt. Most of the seals were of cruciform shape, although there were also square and round varieties, and some in the form of a multi-petalled rosette.

Zoomorphic seals form a special group. Most of these bear repre-sentations of horned domestic animals, although eagles in heraldic poses also occur, as well as a fantastic three-headed animal engraved on the

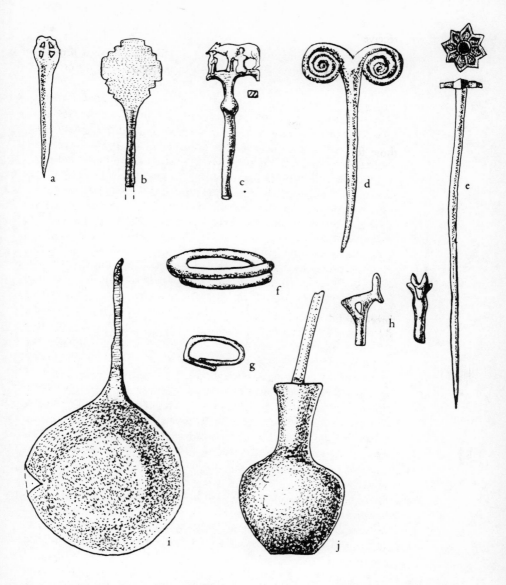

*Fig. 31 Jewellery and metalwork of the Bronze Age from southern Turkmenia. a Yangikalin cemetery;
b, h, i, j Altin-depe; c Khaka hoard, Fergana; d Kizil Arvat; e Ashkhabad cemetery; f, g Auchin-depe*

reverse of a silver seal. The treatment is similar to that used for the zoomorphic designs on Chalcolithic painted pottery.

TRADE

This social specialization may be assumed to have coincided with a significant development of trade. A system of internal exchange will have enabled the inhabitants of the residential quarters of Altin-depe to receive the products of the potters and the other professional craftsmen. It is of course difficult to judge the extent of this exchange, but on the evidence provided by the Geoksyur cemetery, as far back as the Late Chalcolithic period certain clans had specialized in the production of certain commodities. It is very likely that exchange played an important part in supplying small agricultural villages with the products of the specialist crafts.

There is more information on the development of external trade, concerning which two hoards uncovered at Altin-depe proved particularly useful. One of these contained a grey-ware vessel identical with those found at Hissar. Since grey-ware was not produced at all in southern Turkmenia in the Namazga V period, there is no doubt that this was an import from northern Iran. Both hoards also contained objects of Indian ivory comprising square and oval-shaped gaming counters and small sticks of rectangular cross-section, with circles on three sides and a decorative design on the fourth. Numerous objects of this kind were found in the ancient Indian capital of Mohenjo-daro. Similar sticks are also described in Sanskrit texts as part of the equipment used in telling fortunes. It is, therefore, not surprising that many of the pottery forms of Namazga V type have analogies in the Harappan assemblages. There are also analogies of metal artifacts; for example, flat daggers without a midrib which were quite atypical for Hissar, were very widespread both in southern Turkmenia and in the Indus Valley. It must also have been Indian influence which inspired the

Plate 46

three-headed monster which occurs on the silver seal from Altin-depe. It seems very likely that trade was the motivating force behind these connections between India and Central Asia, which became much more marked in the Middle Bronze Age.[4] Important recent evidence indicates the south-westerly, predominantly seaward, direction of the Harappan trade routes. The Harappan influence observed in southern

Turkmenia, however, also indicates trade routes going northwest. It was apparently largely this northern trade of Harappa which led to the rise of Mundigak in southern Afghanistan, which was located advantageously to control the supply of copper and lapis lazuli going to the towns of the Indus Valley. The close resemblance between the unpainted pottery of southern Turkmenia, Seistan and southern Afghanistan is no coincidence. In Mundigak, this similarity with the Turkmenian sites extends to metal seals as well as to seals made of stone and baked clay, with their incised designs.

The problem of contacts between Iran and Mesopotamia and southern Turkmenia in the Middle Bronze Age has not been so widely studied, but significant parallels with Hissar, Shah-tepe, and with Mesopotamia where the south Turkmenian clay figurines and monumental structures are concerned indicate close contacts between these countries. Here, too, trade seems to have played an important part in the diffusion of material culture. It is possible that the most enterprising traders of Sumer and Babylon actually came to these remote outposts of the world of commerce of the day.

There is reason to believe that there were trade routes extending from the South Turkmenian proto-urban communities far to the north, into regions inhabited by 'backward barbarians'. While it is difficult to judge whether these trade connections formed a chain of exchanges with many links, or whether courageous merchants actually travelled over long distances from the southern communities, there is no doubt that such contacts existed and that they played a big part in the spread throughout Central Asia of many cultural developments and discoveries.

The Zaman-baba culture, which has been discovered in the lower reaches of the Zeravshan and is dated to the late third or early second millennium BC, is particularly interesting in this respect. A settlement was excavated in this region comprising semi-subterranean dwellings and a cemetery consisting of single and paired burials in pits and stone chambers. These features, as well as the crude, hand-made pottery, show that Zaman-baba is an early culture of the Steppe Bronze Age. At the same time, the forms of the beads, the bronze pins, the presence of pottery kilns, and a flat baked clay figurine indicate strong influence from the southern Turkmenian communities. Sherds of pottery identical to that of Namazga IV type have also been found and must have been

Fig. 32

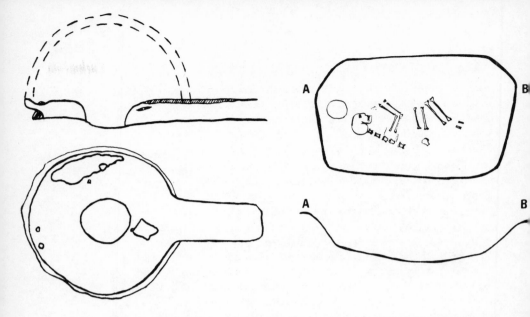

Fig. 32 Material of the Zaman Baba culture. Above, semi-subterranean dwelling and burial type; below, pottery and figurine; right, artifacts of flint, metal and bone, beads, clay oven and clay weights

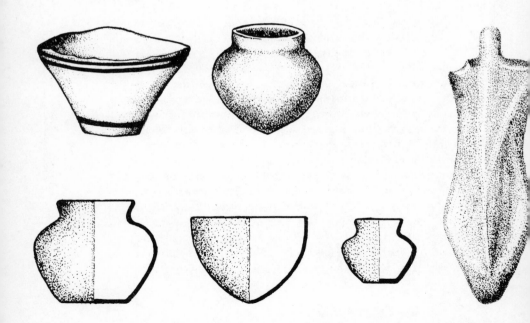

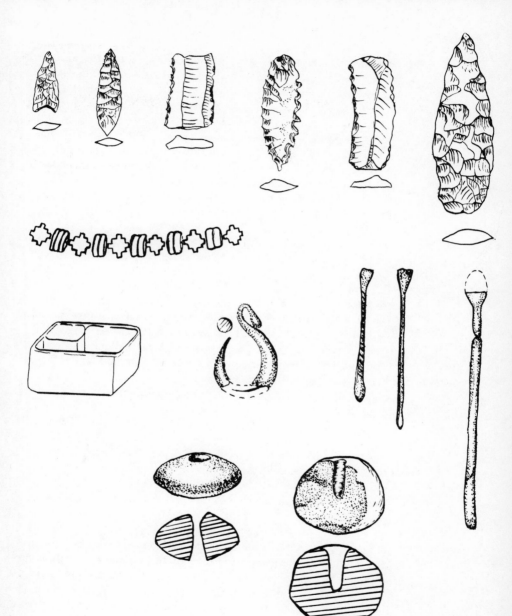

imported. It is very likely that these close contacts with areas where a settled, agricultural way of life had long been established stimulated the transition to a production economy in the lower Zeravshan. At the settlement of Zaman⁄baba grain impressions of wheat and barley were found, as well as bones of domestic animals such as goats, sheep, cows, and asses. The bones of wild animals account for only 15% of the total, which definitely shows that stock⁄breeding and cultivation were established here. The Kelteminar culture of the lower Zeravshan, of which the Zaman⁄baba culture seems to have been an offshoot, is there⁄fore a good example of a 'secondary centre' of the 'Neolithic revolution', in which the transition took place under the strong influence of highly developed centres.

A strong incentive for the merchants from southern Turkmenia may well have been the tin deposits in the area of Bukhara and the Fergana Valley. It is interesting to note that the bronze artifacts found at Zaman⁄baba, although they imitated southern models in shape, were smelted from local ores, judging from the rare impurities in their constitution. The chain of imports from the south continues towards Fergana. The next such point after Zaman⁄baba was Pendjikent, where an adze of the type found at Daina was discovered. At Fergana itself was found a hoard which included some particularly interesting pins with elaborate heads, including a double⁄spiral and a representation of a cow being milked. The southern influence, or perhaps even the southern origin of these articles seems certain.

Fig. 31

We see then that the settled, agricultural communities of southern Turkmenia in the Middle Bronze Age comprised societies with a com⁄plex and highly developed economic structure, with crafts as a special sphere of production on the one hand, and agriculture on the other, the very existence of this division suggesting an internal exchange system growing into trade as an essential link in the economic system as a whole.

SOCIAL ORGANIZATION

In general, however, archaeological evidence presents only limited opportunities for the study of social organization in this period. Judging from all the information available, the large clan was still the primary unit of society. An indication of this is the collective tomb at Altin⁄depe, where fourteen adults were buried successively in a small chamber, the previous internments having in some instances been unceremoniously shoved aside in the process. It would be natural to interpret this as a desire to preserve and emphasize even after death the close kinship ties that bound these people on earth. The number of bodies is an indication that this was not a small, nuclear family, but a larger group. A clay female figurine found in the grave seems to have been the 'house goddess', or icon. It is interesting to note that only two of the bodies had a seal at the waist, and these may well have belonged to the elders of the clan. Yet the clear division of dwellings into small, detached complexes in the residential quarter on the 'Mound of the wall' at Altin-depe indicates the growing importance of the small nuclear family, which began to acquire a more independent economic status.

The seals are an important pointer where social organization is concerned. It is quite clear that they were closely connected with amulet-pendants and the painted pottery of the Chalcolithic period with its symbolic designs. Practically all the basic forms and motifs of these seals have their origin in the various magic symbols of the Late Chalcolithic. Seal impressions on clay in the Middle Bronze Age material indicate one of their functions: thus, one clay figurine of a bull had a brand, a symbol of property, incised on its flank. It is well known that livestock played an important part in the development of the institution of property; since only two seals were found in the collective tomb mentioned above, it is very likely that the valued property was that of the large clan, not personal property. The magic symbol and the good-luck charm were thus transformed into objects protecting property rights.

Doubtless there was a certain amount of property differentiation at Altin-depe as at Namazga-depe; this is borne out by the appearance of hoards, by the wealth of grave offerings and by the presence of more prosperous quarters within the residential areas.

A characteristic feature of the Middle Bronze Age culture of southern Turkmenia was the development of a new type of clay figurine, whose origin goes back to the Early Bronze Age. In contrast to Chalcolithic figurines, where there was an attempt at realistic modelling in the round, the figurines of the Bronze Age were flat and stylized, without any three-dimensional modelling. The female figure now took the form of an elongated frontal silhouette filled in with details, some of which defined the sexual attributes, while others comprised various magical symbols.

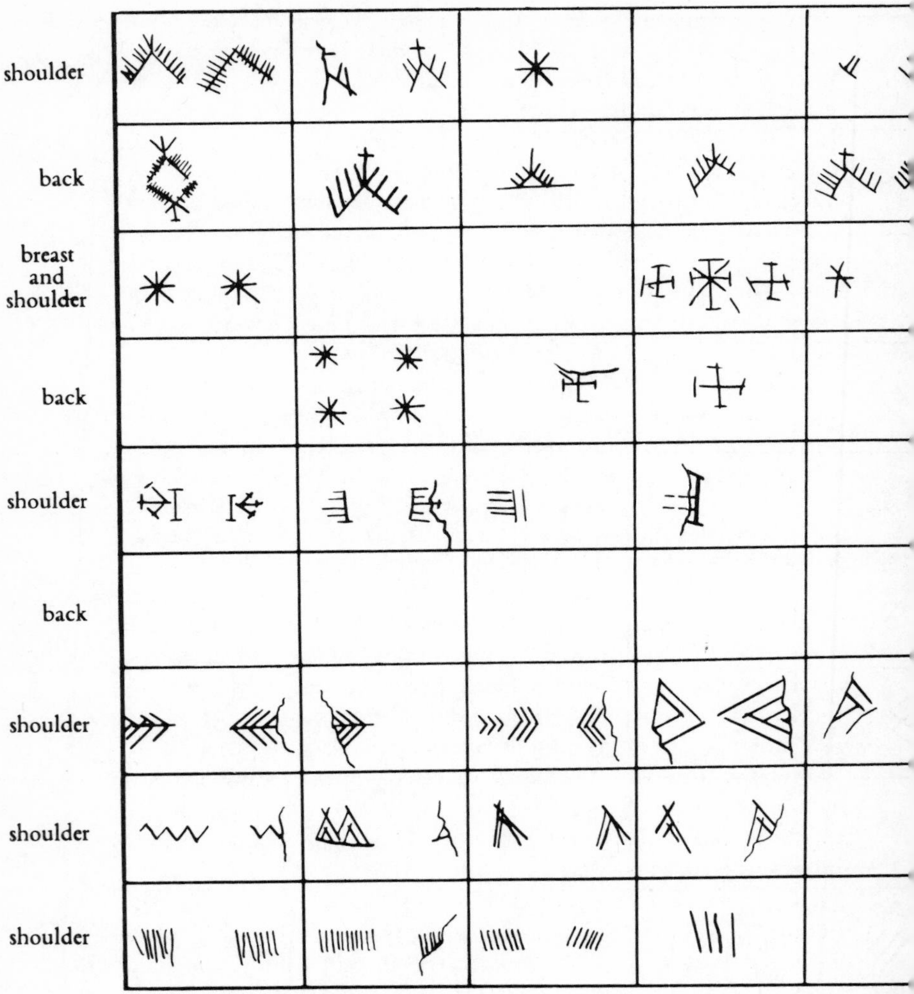

Fig. 33 Motifs scratched on south Turkmenian figurines

Fig. 34 Local prototypes of south Turkmenian motifs

Namazga V		
Namazga IV		
Namazga III		
Namazga II		
Namazga I		
Djeitun		

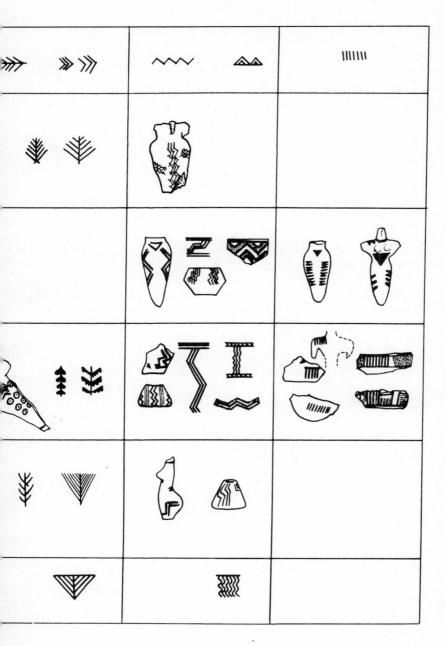

South Turkmenian signs								

Fig. 35   Comparison of south Turkmenian motifs and archaic writing of the Near East

A great deal of attention was given to the depiction of the head, which was attached to a long neck and often crowned with some form of head-dress. The enormous eyes are executed in low relief and produce an almost hypnotic effect. These figures have wide hips and the arms are outstretched. Despite the stylized approach, however, they were still made with great professional skill; this applies particularly to details such as the curling, snake-like plaits framing the face and falling on the breasts, the eyebrows, which were often very carefully portrayed, and the finely notched head-dress which served to offset the arresting eyes. These are further enhanced by various pieces of jewellery at the throat or around the neck. The horizontal incised lines representing girdles en-circling the hips emphasize the willowy vertical lines of the figure itself.

At first glance the replacement of the three-dimensional sculpture of the Chalcolithic by these flat figurines in southern Turkmenia would seem to represent a retrograde step, but there can be no question of any decline in the artistry and skill of the ancient sculptors. The changes des-cribed above apply only to anthropomorphic figurines; the zoomorphic variety continued to be manufactured in the three-dimensional manner, and reveal keen powers of observation as well as a profound knowledge of the habits of each animal.

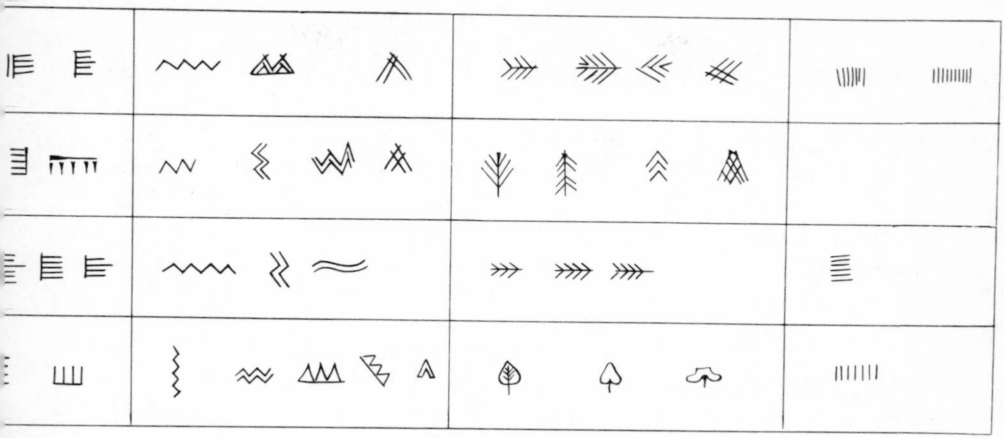

The symbols incised on the front of the shoulders and on the back of the torso of the south Turkmenian clay figurines undoubtedly had a significant meaning. As a result of a preliminary survey, they have been classified into six types. The first type, a triangle with cilia, occurs only on figurines from Altin-depe, where they were very common, distributed all over the settlement. In 1968 a small clay vessel bearing two similar symbols was discovered at Taichanak-depe. The second type, a cruciform star, was more widespread, and occurs on figurines from Altin-depe, Ulug-depe, and Taichanak-depe. The third type, in the form of marks which sometimes resemble the letter 'K', occurs on figurines from three sites: Altin-depe, Khapuz-depe and Taichanak-depe. The fourth type represents a stylized branch of a plant, and has been found at Khapuz-depe and Altin-depe. The fifth (zigzag) type and sixth (row of vertical lines) type are confined to Altin-depe.

The constant repetition of the same symbols is proof that these were no random motifs, nor did they apply only to the semantic aspect of the statue itself. At Altin-depe, where most of the figurines were found, those with identical symbols were more or less equally distributed over the entire settlement. It is most likely that these were the symbols of various gods or female spirits. Thus, figurines with the star symbol might

Fig. 33

Fig. 34

135

represent the god or spirit of the heavens as did Inanna of Sumer, the plant-like branch might well symbolize the spirit of grain, while the zigzag might stand for water.[5] The iconographical differences correlate with these various symbols to some extent. Thus figurines with the triangle and cilia symbol always have a heavy plait hanging down to the waist.

The existence of an established system of symbols, repeatedly used on numerous figurines, naturally leads one to think of writing. Some of the symbols which occur on Middle Bronze Age figurines can be traced back to the symbolism observed in the patterns painted on Chalcolithic pottery. Other symbols seem to have a closer connection with the pictographic writing of Elam and Sumer.[6] The signs on the figurines comprise a set of religious symbols which may have influenced the form-ation of pictographic writing, but did not themselves make up a writing system. It is not impossible that in southern Turkmenia in the Middle Bronze Age a writing system was in the process of formation, but the extent to which it had developed by this time is very difficult to judge. In this connection it is interesting to note that several signs have been found on a fragment of a baked clay tablet. In any case, the occurrence of religious symbols on figurines indicates a high degree of intellectual development of society during the urban revolution. The evolution of abstract thinking, and the economic necessity of keeping regular accounts and systematization were both prerequisites for one of the greatest achievements of human culture—a system of writing.

Thus in the early second millennium BC it is possible to see all the signs of an urban civilization in its formative or early stage in southern Turk-menia. Its rise was the result of the development of the economy and culture of local settled agriculturists of the Chalcolithic period. This civilization, however, developed late (in the late third to early second millennium BC) and never reached the heights of such primary civiliz-ations as Sumer, Babylon, Egypt, and Harappa. It did, however, creatively utilize the achievements and experience accumulated by these more advanced centres.

The fate of this young civilization was dramatic and rather mysterious. Progress in this area was succeeded by a clearly defined period of decline as early as the middle of the second millennium BC. The proto-urban capitals of Altin-depe and Namazga-depe were abandoned, and cultural decay set in.

Fig. 35

Plate 45

CHAPTER IX

Farmers of the Oasis and Nomadic Tribes

Western Central Asia in the middle and second half of the second millennium BC is a good example of the complexity of history and the vagaries of fate. The urban civilization in the south suddenly underwent an abrupt change. The proto-urban capitals of the south went into a decline and were abandoned: the agricultural oases seem to have returned to a period when specialist crafts were just beginning. There is no simple explanation for this phenomenon, but among possible contributing factors would appear to have been an internal crisis in the budding early urban civilization, an agricultural crisis in the submontane belt, or possibly the incursion of certain stock-breeding tribes from outside. Altin-depe was apparently abandoned gradually. Even in the Namazga V period, a number of residential districts already lay in ruins. Neither at Namazga-depe nor at Altin-depe, though, has any trace been discovered of a catastrophic event at the end of the Namazga V period.

The northern areas of Central Asia were inhabited by poor but numerous and apparently warlike tribes of nomadic cattle breeders, whose assemblages archaeologists refer to as the Steppe Bronze Age culture. We shall begin with an examination of the settlements of southern Turkmenia, the traditional agricultural area of Western Central Asia.

Fig. 36

NAMAZGA VI: THE LATE BRONZE AGE

Here the assemblages of Namazga VI type belong to the Late Bronze Age, the beginning of which is marked by the appearance of grey ware and red-slipped pottery, and the end, by hand-made painted pottery of the Yaz I type. Recent excavations at Namazga-depe have revealed a cultural layer of this period with a total thickness of 4.5 m. comprising five building levels, which would indicate that this period was shorter than previous periods.[1] It should evidently be placed within the second half of the second millennium BC, since the upper-most building level of this period at Namazga-depe has been dated by the Carbon 14 method to 1030 ± 60 BC.

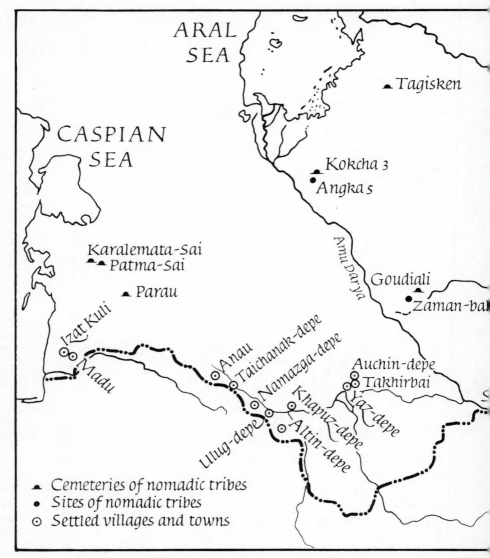

Fig. 36   Distribution of Bronze Age sites in Central Asia

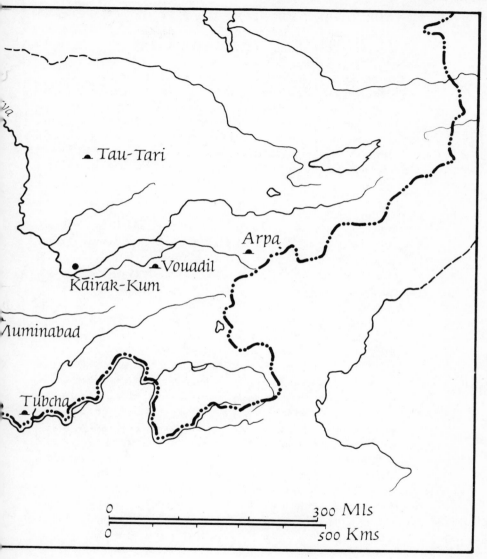

There are two important characteristic features of the oases of southern Turkmenia in this period: the decline of proto-urban centres and the penetration of farmers into a hitherto underdeveloped area, the Murgab Delta. Thus whereas Altin-depe was almost totally abandoned, at Namazga-depe a spark of life remained on only one mound at the northern edge of the settlement. As in the Neolithic period, the agri-cultural villages were small, no larger than a few acres. On the basis of present evidence villages of the Namazga VI period were concentrated in two areas: the submontane zone, where the ancient agricultural settlements lay, and the Murgab Delta. Certain differences are visible in the material culture of these two groups of sites, but these are only slight local variations.

SUBMONTANE ZONE

Settlements of the submontane zone include the south mound at Anau, Elken-depe, and Tekkem-depe. The last named, near Namazga-depe, was probably founded by inhabitants of this former capital in an early stage of its decline. The upper layer of Tekkem-depe contained the remains of several structures which were evidently destroyed by fire, for on the floor were charred fallen rafters.

The largest excavations of a Namazga VI settlement were conducted at Namazga-depe itself. The greater part of the inhabited area of this settlement was abandoned at this time and the remaining population was concentrated in the northern part of the settlement, on the mound (called the 'Bastion') formed by the Namazga VI occupation debris. Next to this sector of Namazga-depe was a cemetery where burial pits were excavated among the ruins of partially collapsed structures of the preceding period. On the 'Bastion' itself three residential blocks divided by streets 2.5–4 m. wide were excavated. Two of these blocks consisted of multi-roomed dwelling complexes built round a central courtyard, or with a courtyard attached, while the third, on the eastern periphery, was rather smaller, and contained the pottery kilns. These kilns were two-tiered, rectangular in plan, with a complex system of heat ducts leading to the firing chambers. This potters' quarter is reminiscent of the traditions of Altin-depe in the Namazga V period, but the scale was completely different: the craftsmen's quarter at Altin-depe in the Middle Bronze Age occupied an area of about 6¼ acres, nearly twice the size of the entire settlement of the 'Bastion'. Such were the visible characteristics of the decline of the southern Turkmenian settlements.

THE MURGAB DELTA

Whereas the Late Bronze Age villages of the submontane belt were generally built on the sites of older settlements, all the Namazga VI villages of the Murgab Delta were founded on new sites. They formed an oasis extending over 43 km. in a north-south direction to the north of the Novy Kishman wells. It is possible that all six villages stood along one of the channels of the old Murgab Delta, each occupying an area of about $2\frac{1}{2}$ to 3 acres. The oldest was probably Auchin-depe, a small mound formed of cultural layers up to 1.5 thick. A two-tiered pottery kiln was excavated at this site comprising a rectangular furnace divided into two by a thin longitudinal wall. This kiln was more primitive than those of the 'Bastion' at Namazga-depe, and on the whole resembled the most common type of pottery kilns of the submontane zone in the preceding period. The village of Takhirbai 3, which occupies an area of about 5 acres is rather later. A courtyard excavated in this village contained a circular kiln and traces of sun-baked brick structures.

In addition to house structures, burials were excavated at most of the settlements. These were exclusively single crouched burials, varying only in the quantity and variety of the grave goods, which usually consisted of pottery and jewellery. (One grave at the 'Bastion' at Namazga-depe contained iron beads). A rich burial excavated in the uppermost layer at Auchin-depe contained 14 vessels, a bronze bracelet, beads of azurite, gypsum, and turquoise, and a stone pendant-seal on which a snake was depicted. An incomplete cremation occurred at one of the Murgab settlements.

Plates, 49, 50

No Late Bronze Age chambers with collective burials have been discovered, but a burial located outside a settlement was found. At the modern village of Yangi-Kala, a cemetery was excavated to the south of Geok-tepe a few kilometres from the possible site of a Late Bronze Age settlement. The burials here were in pits which have since been damaged by erratic streams. The seven excavated graves contained skeletons all lying on the left side with the knees drawn up, but variously orientated. Traces of open fires within the pits may be associated with the burial ceremony. One to four vessels stood either at the head or at the feet, and

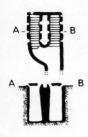

Figs 37, 38   Material of Namazga VI type, Murgab variant. Left, clay oven; right, pottery, clay figurines, seals, and artifacts of metal, stone and bone

Figs 37, 38

two graves contained broken anthropomorphic clay figurines which were made in the style of the preceding periods. One of the burials is rather different in that the grave goods consisted of four vessels, a clay figurine and six pieces of bronze jewellery. The locating of cemeteries outside the settlements seems to have been quite common in the Namazga VI period.

The definite decline which marked the entire Namazga VI period may be seen very clearly in the pottery. Although the basic technical advances of the preceding period were by no means forgotten (both the potter's wheel and the special two-tiered kilns remained in existence) the shape of the vessels became cruder and less varied, and the technique of manufacture was less refined.

The pottery clearly shows the two regional variants; that made in the submontane villages is covered with a light or red slip of various shades, and grey ware is relatively rare. Some of the grey ware and red-slipped vessels were burnished, usually in a vertical direction. The most common form in the submontane region is the pedestalled vase which is sometimes fluted, but conical stands, conical bowls with incurving rims, and large globular vessels with a concave curve at the base are also found. The pottery is generally undecorated, although incised wavy or straight lines and rows of vertical notches occasionally occurred. Globular cooking bowls were made by hand, and their rims are sometimes decorated with slanting notches.

The pottery of the Murgab villages may be divided into two distinct chronological groups. The earlier group, from Auchin-depe, resembles that of the Namazga V complex of the submontane belt; most of it is red or pink ware, with a light-coloured slip. Grey ware occasionally occurs. Vases, some pedestalled, and large globular vessels with a concave or annular base predominate. The later group of pottery, represented by the material from Takhirbai 3, differs much more from that of the submontane belt, probably as a result of the growth of cultural and economic independence in the new oasis, similar to the situation during

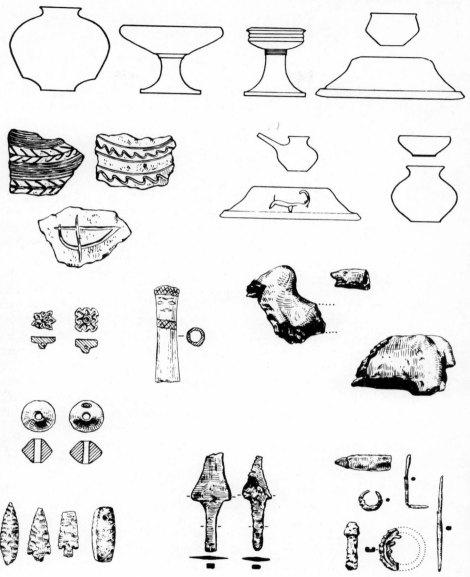

the Chalcolithic period in the Geoksyur Oasis. The Murgab pottery had certain elements in common with the pottery of Namazga-depe: the large globular vessels with a concave curving lower part, annular base, and incised decoration are an example. On the other hand none of the Murgab villages had red burnished bowls with incurving rims; the predominant pottery was goblet-shaped grey ware. The shape of the vases is also different, one of the forms closely resembling the late Harappan style of the Indus Valley. Domestic pots were made by hand, as were disc-shaped shallow dishes. Although pottery of Namazga VI type is common in the material of the settlements of both the submontane belt and the Murgab Delta, there is far less variety of shapes than in the preceding period.

In the manufacture of metal articles we can trace a definite continuation of local traditions, but there are also certain interesting new trends. Southern Turkmenia remained one of the largest metal-producing areas in Central Asia. The basic tool types in the Namazga VI period follow the traditional forms of the Middle Bronze Age, including especially tanged knives and daggers with a flat, wide ridgeless blade as well as awls with a rectangular cross-section, and 'razors' which were probably used as cleavers. In addition to these, another type of tool at Namazga-depe is a sickle-shaped, single-edged knife, which certainly had its analogies in the settlements of the Andronovo culture. This fact is all the more significant since the proper sickles of the Namazga VI period closely resemble those found in settlements further south, particularly in the cemetery of Tepe Sialk A, both in the shape of the tool and in the method of attaching the handle. The Murgab villages produced flat points for darts which resembled in shape the knives of the Catacomb culture. In addition two types of flint arrow-head were in wide use —one of which was a tang-less, laurel-leaf shape, while the other was tanged with two barbs. Bronze jewellery included bracelets, rings, ear-pendants and disc-shaped diadems for wearing on the forehead. As in the Middle Bronze Age, there was a large variety of pins, some of which had openwork heads, others had heads in the form of an eight-petalled rosette, and all now had sharply tapering ends. Sporadic fragments of bronze seals also occur, and stone seals, in the rosette form or in the traditional cruciform shape, were also produced, though zoomorphic seals were discontinued. Large biconical stone beads, usually carved out of steatite and with the surface sometimes decorated with concentric circles, are characteristic of the Namazga VI culture.

Thus implements and jewellery of the Namazga VI period continued the traditions of the Middle Bronze Age, but in the minor arts a certain decline was already apparent. The marvellous clay figurines of the Middle Bronze Age, for example, were succeeded by figures of a disappointingly low standard. Indeed, the whole tradition of making clay figurines, which undoubtedly had a Neolithic origin, was gradually allowed to lapse, so that by the beginning of the Iron Age their manufacture had ceased entirely. The Namazga VI period has yielded only a few fragments of clay animal figurines and mere traces of zoomorphic pots and anthropomorphic figurines. One of these, found in the cemetery at Yangi-Kala, represents a standing woman of a new iconographic type, in that instead of the full-hipped slim-waisted female figure of the Chalcolithic and Middle Bronze Age, this portrays a thin nude female figure with a girdle around her waist. Only the thick braid hanging down her back is reminiscent of the old traditions. A small human figure which was casually scratched on a tubular piece of bone found in the village of Takhirbai 3 has its analogies in the cultures further north, beyond the area of the settled farming cultures. It is interesting to note that the decoration as seen on the clay figurines of Namazga V disappeared in this period. Incised decoration on vessels, especially their pedestals, was quite different and included a goat, and what looks like a bow and arrow, as well as the cross which was a traditional motif in south Turkmenian decoration. In addition, one pedestal from the 'Bastion' of Namazga-depe was decorated by a swastika, which was an absolutely new motif in local symbolism. This sign was never found again in the whole rich collection of south Turkmenian painted pottery.

Even though there were unmistakeable signs of deterioration and decline, southern Turkmenia during the Late Bronze Age remained a region with settled agricultural communities and relatively well-developed crafts. Grains of wheat and barley and grape seeds excavated at Elken-depe show that the basic crops remained the same. At Tekkem-depe the bones of sheep, goat, cow, pig, camel, and possibly horse, provide evidence that no great change took place in the keeping of domestic animals although the Elken-depe material seems to indicate a preponderance of the smaller species. Craft traditions of the Middle

Bronze Age were retained to a certain extent, although on a sharply-reduced scale with a small variety of artifacts and a lower standard of workmanship.

Evidence of continuing trade with the south may be seen in the pins with rosette heads which have analogies in the metal-producing centres of the Near East, the large stone beads decorated by concentric circles which were known in Hissar-III-C and in the post-Harappan complexes of Jukar, and certain pottery forms which show Indian influence.

At the same time there seems to have been some form of contact also with the north. We have already mentioned the sickle-shaped knife from Namazga-depe which is very similar to those of the Andronovo culture. In addition, there is evidence in the Murgab villages of the Namazga VI period of the rite of partial cremation, which is also known in a number of the Steppe Bronze Age cultures. The question therefore arises whether some northern influence might account for the appearance of cemeteries, such as that at Yangi-Kala, which lay apart from the settlement, whereas in earlier periods settlements and burials were generally found on the same site. It is interesting to note in this connection that at Takhirbai 3 a skull was discovered which has proto-European features, morphologically similar to the types of Bronze Age skulls from the Volga, southern Siberia and the Altai region. Sherds of Andronovo type, found at several villages of the Namazga VI period provide evidence of direct contact between the farmers and the descendants of nomads. Behind this scattered evidence may well lie hidden historic events of paramount significance. Before proceeding to possible interpretations, however, we should examine briefly the northern regions of Western Central Asia.

NORTHERN ZONE: THE STEPPE BRONZE AGE

Here the southern origin of the steppe cultures is very clear. Behind the apparent homogeneity of these steppe cultures there seems to lie a very complex situation in which coexistence and mutual assimilation of tribes of different origins and with different ethnocultural contacts took place. Basically, there are three important cultural and territorial groups of sites. Firstly, the group of burials of the Timber-Grave (Srubnaya) culture in western Turkmenia, secondly, the very large group, or perhaps even several groups of sites belonging to the Androvono

Fig. 39   Burial of the Andronovo culture

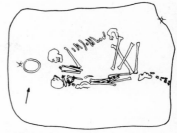

culture group, and finally, the unusual and very interesting group of sites on the shore of the Caspian Sea, where the conditions of the steppe-dwellers most closely resembled those of the settled agricultural zone of the south.

In this region several cemeteries have been discovered to the north of Balkhan. In the Bronze Age, this desert region was evidently fairly well developed by a stock-breeding population, whose existence is attested only by these burial sites. They comprise small barrows covered with stones to keep the earth in place, with a grave pit dug under the barrow and covered with stone slabs, on which there are occasionally traces of camp fires. The body was laid on its left side in a crouched position, the head towards the east. The grave goods found in the excavated barrows were rather poor, consisting of crude hand-made pots and the remains of a wooden vessel. The rites adopted, and the vessels themselves, show strong influence from the Timber-Grave culture suggesting that these burials represent a local variant of this very large cultural complex, which has been studied in detail in the Volga basin and the Ukraine. The Balkhan sites in Turkmenia are by no means unique, for similar burials occur in three cemeteries to the west of Kizil Arvat in which the skeleton was again laid on its left side, with the head towards the east. An additional point of interest is that one of the barrows seems to have been surmounted by a rather complicated structure made up of two rings of stones. There is no doubt that these sites also belong to the Steppe Bronze Age culture, up till now represented only in eastern Europe.

The sites of the Andronovo culture in Western Central Asia, however, are by no means all alike. In those of the ancient delta of the Amu-Darya, in the cemetery of Kokcha-3, for example, no traces of tombstones remain; if the graves had a wooden marker or construction, this has not been preserved. The body was buried in a shallow pit, the bottom of which was sometimes lined with rushes, invariably in a con-

Fig. 39

147

Fig. 40 Pottery and metalwork from sites of Andronovo type

tracted position with the head nearly always towards the west. A curious distinction is made according to sex, the males being laid on their right side, the females on their left. Double graves occur, in some of which the subsequent, second burial disturbed the skeletal arrangement of the first. In three cases the first to be buried was a man, in three others a woman. As a rule, these were persons of approximately the same age, and it is possible that we have here family vaults. This hypothesis is supported by the fact that three of the double burials included children. Similar burial rites occur in the Steppe Bronze Age cultures of Eurasia, and would seem to indicate the separate existence of a 'small' or 'nuclear' family (man, wife, children) within a larger family unit or clan.[2] The grave-goods in the burials, comprising a few pottery vessels placed at the head, and jewellery of various kinds including beads of bronze, paste and sardonyx, with bracelets and pendants for the women, lacked variety.

Thus the assemblages in the cemetery of Kokcha-3 have close parallels in the Steppe Bronze Age culture of more northerly regions, and there are enough similarities in the basic shapes and decoration of the pottery to enable it to be assigned to the Ala-kul stage of the Andronovo culture as seen in west Kazakhstan.

Along with these analogies there is some resemblance between the Amu-Darya pottery and that of the Timber-Grave culture of the Volga, which is yet another variety of the Steppe Bronze Age. Apart from general similarities, there are certain finds which connect the lower reaches of the Amu-Darya directly to the Steppe Bronze Age; the temporal pendants found in the cemetery at Kokcha-3, for example, are of the same kind as those of the Volga Timber-Grave culture. A propos these and other bronze artifacts from the Amu-Darya sites, it is significant that these sites are located very near to the metal ore

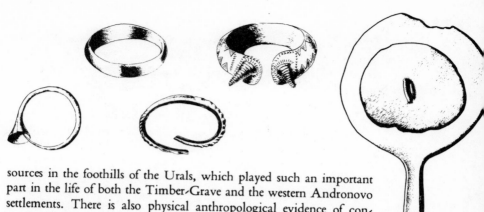

sources in the foothills of the Urals, which played such an important part in the life of both the Timber-Grave and the western Andronovo settlements. There is also physical anthropological evidence of connections between the lower Amu-Darya and the Timber-Grave sites of the Volga. Tolstov and others have concluded that these sites of the lower reaches of the Amu-Darya represent a separate culture, referred to as the Tazagabiab culture. Another view is that they represent a local variant (the Tazagabiab variant) of the Andronovo culture, and on the basis of the available evidence, this latter hypothesis would seem preferable.

The economy of these Tazagabiab settlements is of great interest. The bones of cows, sheep and, occasionally, horses have been excavated, showing that the people were stock-breeders. In addition the clay figure of a horse was found with a hole through its mane which suggests that it was part of a model horse-drawn cart. The wheels from such a model have also been excavated in the Tazabagiab settlements. Besides stock-breeding, there is evidence of extensive agriculture in the very favourable conditions of the shrinking delta.[3] Traces of irrigation ditches were found some 150–200 m. from several side channels of the delta. When a channel of this sort finally dried up, a special canal was dug alongside it repeating all its bends, in order to take water to the fields. Along these existing and ancient channels stood the villages themselves, comprising 3–10 rectangular semi-subterranean dwellings, each 50–80 sq. m. The roofs of the houses were supported by wooden posts and a large rectangular hearth occupied the centre of the room. From its size, such a structure could have served as a dwelling for a number of families, possibly related, forming a single household. Surface-based houses of wattle and daub, however, such as those used in the agricultural settlements further south, were as yet unknown here.

The Steppe Bronze Age material from the lower reaches of the Zeravshan was very similar to that of the sites of Khorezm. Early in the second millennium BC this was the area of the Zaman-baba culture, but in the second half of that millennium this same territory was occupied by a number of settlements belonging to the Tazabagiab variant of the Andronovo culture. Of particular interest was the evidence from the Gudjaili cemetery: as at Kokcha-3 no tombstones were found and the bodies were placed on their left side in a contracted position, the head towards the west. Temporal pendants almost identical with those of the Amu-Darya sites were found. The discovery of metal slag testifies to local metalworking, but in shape the artifacts from Gudjaili resemble those of the southern Urals. Higher up along the Zeravshan, at Mumin-abad in the Samarkand oasis, several burials of this period were excavated. One of these contained rich grave-goods comprising four bracelets decorated with gold leaf, a bronze mirror, over a thousand beads, and socketed temporal rings.

The cultural affiliations of the sites of the Tashkent oasis are more complex; here a number of isolated burials have been found, as well as metal artifacts both in hoards, and singly. Some profess to see a resemblance between these burials and those of the Timber-Grave culture. A heavy-butted axe from the Chimbailyk hoard reveals the strong influence of the southern Ural metal centres. On the other hand, bracelets with spiral terminals would indicate connections with eastern and central Kazakhstan. An extremely interesting find in this connection is a cremation burial in which the body was accompanied by a richly decorated vessel. This was common in Kirghizia in this period.

A number of features which are typical of the Steppe Bronze Age, have been found in sites in this latter area; they point to the existence of another variant of the Andronovo culture, known as the Tien-shen variant, and the Semirechensk (Seven Rivers) variant. It is characterized by the cemeteries excavated in the valley region of northern Kirghizia, in which the burials were marked on the surface by a rectangular enclosure of large stone slabs. The sides of the burial pit were also sometimes lined with stone slabs, or sometimes with clay, and the bodies were cremated, only the ashes being buried. The crude hand-made pottery in the graves was generally undecorated. The graves also contained bronze bracelets, ear-rings made of bronze or silver covered in gold leaf, and a large number of plates, rings and beads of various kinds, which were apparently sewn on to the clothing. No fewer than 1,300 such beads made of bronze, paste, and antimony were found in a single grave. One cemetery in the Tien-Shen, in the Arpa Valley, was located at an altitude of about 2,800 m. above sea level, which may indicate seasonal pasturing on alpine meadows. On the whole, the Kirghiz material was very close to the Ala-Kul phase of the Andronovo culture in the period of its development. The forms of the metal artifacts also point to clear influence from the metal-producing centres of Kazakhstan.

These same Andronovo features are very clear in the material from Fergana, where at one time it was thought there might have been a separate Kairak-Kum Bronze Age culture.[4] It may in the future be possible to isolate a Fergana variant of the Andronovo culture, in which case it would be more correct to call it the Kairak-Kum variant. A group of sites, referred to as the Kairak-Kum group, have been excavated on the right bank of the Syr-Darya between Leninabad and Kanibadam. The cultural layer at these sites has been largely destroyed, but ex-cavations have revealed the remains of hearths, metal slag, and a mould for casting the heavy-butted axe of the Kazakhstan type. The pottery is decorated with pit and comb impressions and shows influence from the Andronovo pottery. The dead were buried in stone cists but, in contrast to the Kirghiz burials, were not cremated. Two other cemeteries— Vuadil and Karam-Kul, both located in the vicinity of Fergana—had some sort of connection with Kairak-Kum. As in Kirghizia, the graves in these cemeteries were marked with rectangular or oval stone enclosures but, as in Kairak-Kum, the bodies were inhumed, not cremated.

The fourth local variant of the Andronovo culture is found in south-west Tadjikistan. A number of cemeteries excavated in this region indicate a sequence of three cultures of the Steppe Bronze Age. The earliest of these, probably dating to about the fifteenth or fourteenth century BC, is represented by cremation burials in small pits. A supple-mentary depression which was dug at the bottom of the pit to hold the cremated remains of the dead, was covered over with fragments of stone slabs, and next to it a pattern of stones was laid out in the form of a circle with an inscribed cross, or swastika. Small sherds of crude hand-made pottery are of Steppe Bronze Age type, but a more exact dating is scarcely possible.

In the second culture, the dead were buried in a shallow pit which was approached by a sloping path, so that the grave was in some respects an imitation of an earthen shelter, a kind of 'last dwelling place'. The bodies were inhumed in a crouched position, mostly with the head towards the east or the west. As in the cemetery at Kokcha-3, all the female skeletons were found lying on the left side, the males on the right: 'paired' burials, too, have been found, as in the cemeteries of the lower reaches of the Amu Darya. At the bottom of these burial pits, shallow stone-lined depressions filled with cinders and ashes were found which could have been a kind of hearth enhancing the simulation of a home. In graves assigned to one sex only the shape of these hearths differed, those in women's graves being round, and those in men's, square. The grave goods exemplify the cultural traditions of the archaic complexes of both the Steppe Bronze Age culture and the settled agriculturists. Most of the pottery consists of hand-made vessels, including globular pots, but elegant wheel-turned pottery has also been found. The metal artifacts include traditional southern shapes (oval mirrors without handles, 'razors', pins with bi-spiral heads) and knives of northern type. All this material has enabled us to date these graves to the ninth/eighth centuries BC. The fact that the graves are situated outside the agricultural area, the discovery of the bones of domesticated sheep, and the general aspect of this culture indicate that these were the sites of nomadic tribes who had come in contact with settled agriculturists whose culture in many ways resembled that of Namazga VI.[5] At the same time the originality of these sites in south-western Tadjikistan justifies the identification of a Steppe Bronze Age culture which is known as the Bishkent culture. It is worth noting that in the valleys of the Vakhsh and the Kafirnigan, where sites of the Bishkent culture were distributed, graves of catacomb type dating back to the early first millennium BC have been discovered and indicate that this area may have been settled by yet another group of people.

One of the most important underlying features of this period is the wide distribution of people who had adopted the Steppe Bronze Age cultures. Opinions on this point vary, some authorities insisting that this culture was of purely local origin,[6] others that it resulted from infiltration by a people representing the Andronovo culture into Western Central Asia via Kazakhstan. It is possible, however, that this complex was the result of the spread of certain tribal groups and their partial assimilation of

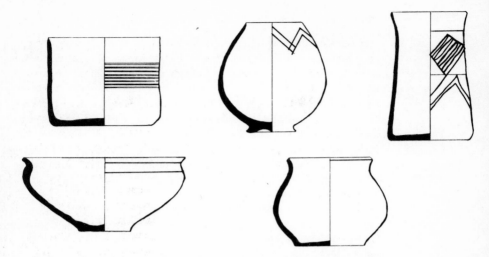

the local population.[7] This would explain why the ethnic composition of Western Central Asia was generally so varied in the Late Bronze Age. At the same time the migration of tribal groups to the south is an almost established fact. The second millennium BC was a period of great migrations and population changes, possibly as a result of the 'population explosion' in the Euro-Asian steppes following the adoption of nomadic stock-breeding and primitive agriculture which replaced the archaic Neolithic economy. At all events, the archaeological material at our disposal leaves no doubt as to the spread of a population with Andronovo and Timber-Grave culture characteristics. There were two main movements of these steppe tribes into Western Central Asia. The sources of the first were the Timber-Grave culture of the Volga area and the West Kazakhstan variant of the Andronovo culture. These have their analogies in the Timber-Grave culture of western Turkmenia and the Tazabagiab variant in the lower reaches of the Amu Darya and the Zeravshan rivers, and had a marked influence on the Tashkent Oasis. In addition, there was a close association between the Timber-Grave culture and some of the sites of the western Andronovo culture, which have a large number of Timber-Grave culture elements including their physical anthropological type.[8]

The second movement stems from the Andronovo traditions of Central and Eastern Kazakhstan, analogies of which have been found in

Kirghizia and the Fergana Valley, though in the middle reaches of the River Zeravshan these apparently met the opposite stream of the Timber-Grave western Kazakhstan Andronovo influence (the Muminabad cemetery).

This should, of course, be studied in conjunction with the problem of the diffusion of tribes of the Indo-Iranian linguistic group. It is known that the first mention of gods with Indo-Iranian names occurs in the Mesopotamian written records of the fourteenth century BC, and the oldest parts of the *Rig-Veda* are apparently of the same date. Toponymic studies clearly show that in the ninth to the seventh centuries BC Iranian tribes appeared in large numbers in Eastern Media and later moved west. It is quite logical to assume that Western Central Asia was also affected by this process, especially if, as was mentioned in the *Avesta* and other sources, an Iranian-speaking population predominated here in the first half of the first millennium BC. Some authorities believe that the sites of the Timber-Grave culture, as well as the west Kazakhstan variant of the Andronovo culture, are undoubtedly associated with an Iranian-speaking population in that it would seem that they evolved into a population which in the Scythian period was Iranian-speaking. A similar conclusion could be made with regard to certain at least of the east Andronovo population which laid the foundations of the Iranian-speaking Sachian culture. These comparisons suggest that the great migrations in the second millennium BC were connected with the spread of the Indo-Iranian tribes and smaller tribal groups accompanying them. It is worth noting in this respect that there are certain parallels between the burial rites of the Steppe Bronze Age culture and the burial rites described in the *Rig-Veda*.[9]

Naturally, the question remains of the fate of the advanced agricultural population which had long been living in the south of Western Central Asia. It may be that it was partly assimilated by the newcomers during the Namazga VI period when it can be seen that the local culture adopted certain 'steppe' features, for example, the swastika, which had been unknown here before. A new physical anthropological type also appears to emerge. At the same time the newcomers may have adopted the advanced culture of the local population, much as the urban population of Western Central Asia in the twelfth to the seventeenth centuries AD absorbed Turkish influence.

CHAPTER X

Canals and Fortresses : the Early Iron Age

In the Early Iron Age in Western Central Asia, the situation was no less complex. In this period there is no lack of archaeological evidence: the only problem is in finding a satisfactory interpretation.

As in the preceding chapters, we shall begin our survey with the ancient agricultural region of south-western Central Asia, where in the late second and early first millennia BC two different cultures developed. The first of these was the Dakhistan culture, whose most important sites were located on the Misrian plain; it derived its name from the Dakhi tribes that populated it in ancient times. The second culture was distributed in the old agricultural centres on the submontane plain of the Kopet Dag and in the Murgab river delta.

THE DAKHISTAN CULTURE

The Dakhistan culture is represented by small settlements located near *Figs 43, 44* the modern towns of Bami, Beurme, and Kizil Arvat. The largest oasis, however, is on the Misrian plain (Turkoman Steppe) near the south-eastern shore of the Caspian Sea, while a number of villages sites have been found in the valley of the River Sumbar.

So far the most extensively studied are the sites on the Misrian plain. These include small settlements an acre or so in area, and great cities, the ruins of which cover an area of 100 acres or more (Izat Kuli, Madau-depe, Chialyk-depe, Tangsikyldja). The plan of these cities is very interesting. Izat Kuli, for example, with an area of nearly 125 acres, had a pentagonal fortress at its centre. A similar plan was discovered at Madu-depe, in which the central fortress reached a height of 13.5 m. (the thickness of the entire cultural layer of the city itself is only 6.5 m.). Partial excavations showed that the fortress was built on a platform made of sun-baked brick and located around it were multi-roomed dwelling complexes. Near Madu-depe and Izat Kuli were found the remains of canals 50–60 km. in length; these may have led from channels of the delta of the River Atrek, indicating the existence of large irrigation systems on the Misrian plain as early as the end of the second or the beginning of the first millennium BC, if not earlier.

The wheel-turned pottery of the Dakhistan culture is distinguished by its very high quality of workmanship. Most of it is grey ware, often black-slipped and undecorated but carefully burnished. There is a smaller amount of red and light-green pottery. Typical vessels include jugs, cups with a sophisticated curved shape (beak), and censers in the form of a spherical bowl on a tall, hollow pedestal.

Although no iron artifacts have yet been found, their existence may well be inferred from the presence of fragments of iron slag and casting moulds.[1] The finds include leaf-shaped bronze arrow-heads with a tang and two or three barbs, and at Madu-depe a bronze sword. In spite of the fairly large variety of metal objects, flint blades for sickles were frequently found. There were also stone artifacts such as querns, poun-ders, grindstones, and missiles for slings. It is likely that there was still a metal shortage at this time so that stone tools were generally used for domestic purposes. One object of interest was a square table with short legs and a drain, which may have had a sacrificial use.

The Dakhistan culture at this time was characterized by agriculture and stock-breeding, with a fairly high standard of living and with a ruling minority living in the fortified 'citadels'. The complex irrigation systems called for centralized management. According to one perfectly plausible theory, the population of the Misrian plain formed a union of communities, in which the beginnings of a state can already be seen.

The origins of the Dakhistan culture pose an extremely interesting question, for on the basis of the available evidence it would seem to have appeared in an already developed form. However, very similar material evidence is found in the Caspian regions of northern Iran. Indeed, the pottery of these two areas is in many cases absolutely identical; for example the grey ware vessels with elaborate curved beaks, whose exact copies are to be found in the pottery of such villages as Shah-tepe (sector IIa), Tureng-tepe, Hissar III, and to a lesser extent Tepe

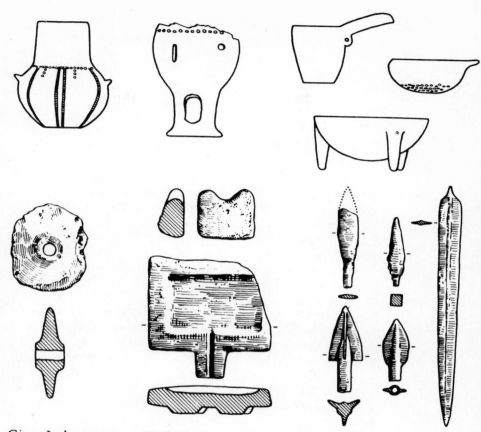

Giyan I, the cemetery at Sialk B, Kalar Dashta and Kurvin. The similarity is so obvious that it has been suggested that there was a genetic connection between the pottery of ancient Dakhistan and that of Shah-tepe. In the light of these comparisons, there is every reason to believe that the Misrian plain was settled and developed as a result of colonization from northern Iran. As yet it is difficult to say whether this was a gradual settlement aimed at developing new lands or whether it was caused by some political events which gave rise to the Dakhistan culture in south-western Turkmenia. In fact, if we accept the usual chronological framework, there was a difference of several hundred years between the abandonment of the south Iranian settlements such as Shah-tepe and

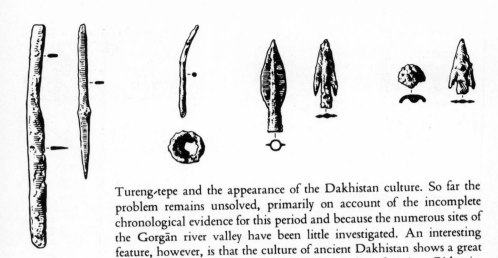

Tureng-tepe and the appearance of the Dakhistan culture. So far the problem remains unsolved, primarily on account of the incomplete chronological evidence for this period and because the numerous sites of the Gorgān river valley have been little investigated. An interesting feature, however, is that the culture of ancient Dakhistan shows a great resemblance, culturally and economically, to that of ancient Girkania, referred to in the *Avesta* and the Achaemenian inscriptions.

SOUTH-EAST TURKMENIA: THE YAZ I COMPLEX

Fig. 45

Let us turn now to the sites of south-eastern Turkmenia, where the archaeological assemblages of the late second and early first millennia BC are characterized by predominantly hand-made pottery, often with painted decoration, the appearance of the first artifacts of iron and double-barbed socketed arrow-heads of bronze, as well as the incidence of large settlements with fortresses on high platforms. This culture was first and most thoroughly studied at the large settlement of Yaz-depe in the Murgab Delta, where it is represented by Yaz-depe I. The beginning of Yaz I is characterized primarily by the almost complete disappearance of Late Bronze Age wheel-made pottery (Namazga VI culture) and the diffusion of hand-made painted ware.

The Yaz I complex at the settlement of Yaz-depe itself has been dated to 900–650 BC. The earliest phases were not found here, but they seem to have been identified at another settlement, Elken-depe, where the Yaz I complex there is dated as a whole from the twelfth to the seventh centuries BC.

The sites of Yaz I type are divided territorially into two groups. One group is distributed in the submontane belt of the Kopet Dag, located in ancient agricultural oases. At the beginning of the first millennium BC

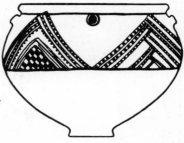

Fig. 45   Yaz I-type assemblage: bronze artifacts and pottery

this region may be designated northern Parthia. Here, in addition to the small villages of the type found on the southern mound at Anau (layer Anau IV), large settlements covering more than 25 acres have been found, with fortified citadels raised on platforms many metres high.

Among these is Elken-depe (which means 'Great Mound'), located 15 km. east of the ancient agricultural capital of Namazga-depe. At this site a fortified citadel stands on a high platform in the centre of the settlement, which has led some researchers to believe that this was a true city. Excavations showed that a small settlement on this site was founded as early as the Late Bronze Age, but cultural layers of Yaz I type in some places lie on bedrock, indicating rapid growth of the settlement at this time. There is no doubt that Elken-depe was a large centre, possibly even the capital of northern Parthia early in the first millennium BC.

Another settlement of the submontane belt—Ulug-depe—was rather smaller in size. It was earlier thought to have had a town wall, but excavations showed that the outskirts of the settlement contained no walls, but ordinary dwellings. It has been established that early in the first millennium BC Ulug-depe was a major centre; Elken-depe and Ulug-depe were, in fact, the largest and most important settlements of their time in the foothills of Kopet Dag, all the rest would appear to have been small agricultural villages.

The second territorial group was made up of two medium oases in the Murgab Delta, in the region that has been named, in various sources, Margiana. The western oasis has several unimportant villages grouped around a central settlement, Arvali-depe, while in the eastern oasis the central settlement was Yaz-depe, which may have been the local capital. It is supposed that both agricultural oases were dependent on a system of canals leading off the main stream of the River Murgab.

Fig. 46

The settlement of Yaz-depe, some 35 km. north-west of the modern town of Bairam Ali, even today gives an impression of majesty and grandeur. It covers an area of 40 acres, the citadel in the centre rising to a height of 12 m., of which 8 m. comprises a solid platform of sun-baked bricks. The citadel alone occupies an area of about 2½ acres, or nearly the entire inhabited area of the southern mound at Anau in the same period. It was possibly fortified with towers, and had a central entrance; in its southern section a large building was excavated which consisted of a number of long rooms with a vaulted roof made of sun-baked brick. Adjacent to this was the central hall, about 26 m. × 7 m., which may have been either a temple or a palace. Originally this building had an upper storey which may have served as a tower. Some 200 sling-stones were recovered here indicating that in the last period this was probably also the citadel garrison. In the settlement itself were multi-roomed dwellings for the ordinary people, while on the periphery were the craftsmen's shops and the potters' kilns.

Among the objects found at Yaz-depe and a number of other settlements, certainly the most interesting are the fragments of an iron sickle excavated on the southern mound at Anau. This is perhaps the most ancient iron artifact to be found so far in all Western Central Asia. Still being widely used at this time were bronze implements such as knives and augers, as well as double-barbed arrow-heads of two types, some with sockets and others tanged; also bronze appliqué ornaments for sewing on clothing. Other finds included a bone bit, and spherical maceheads, mortars, pounders, querns, and door sockets—all made of stone.

The typical pottery of Yaz I type was hand-made, showing a complete break with Bronze Age traditions. In the oldest layers of the Yaz I culture only 5.5% of vessels were made on the potter's wheel; later the figure reaches 14.5%, but even this is a very small proportion. It should be noted, however, that the small percentage of wheel-made pottery has direct connections with the preceding Late Bronze Age pottery. This is strikingly illustrated at such settlements in north Bactria as Elken-depe and Ulug-depe, where the earlier stages of the complex under review are represented: many of the vases and goblets, some red-slipped, some of grey-ware and frequently burnished, are identical to those of the Late Bronze Age in Namazga VI.

The hand-made pottery may be divided into three smaller groups. The first consists of painted pottery, mostly in the form of bowls and pot-bellied vessels. The patterns are mostly geometric and often rather intricate; they were applied with reddish-brown or less often greenish paint. The variety of patterns at Yaz-depe is much poorer than at Elken-depe and Ulug-depe where they include many entirely new designs. The second pottery group comprises the grey-ware, often carefully burnished, in the shape of bowls and pots, the latter usually having looped handles at the rim, while the third group contains unpainted light-slipped bowls and *chymoi*, cooking pots and dishes.

Plate 51

The problem of the origins of Yaz I pottery has been studied in great detail, but no firm conclusions have yet been reached. Schmidt considered pottery of the Anau IV type to be connected with some sort of 'barbarian' invasion, and proposed that that entire period be named the 'age of the barbarian occupation'. The adherents of this theory see such 'coarse' Yaz I type pottery as the result of a strong 'barbaric' influence on the local culture due to the invasion of steppe tribes from the north. Since, however, the Steppe Bronze Age tribes did not have pottery of the Yaz I type, a compromise interpretation has been put forward, namely, that the painted decoration was an imitation of the pottery of the Steppe Bronze Age.

And indeed, many of the new motifs at Ulug-depe recall the decoration on Steppe Bronze Age incised pottery. Yet even this evidence presents no solution to the general problem; for it does not explain why the steppe tribes, having occupied the agricultural centres, should have given up their traditional incising technique and begun painting their pottery—a practice which had ceased among those same agricultural tribes of southern Turkmenistan a thousand years earlier.

On the other hand, recent studies have widened the distribution area of the Yaz I culture, as is borne out by the material from Kuchuk-tepe, near the town of Termez in southern Uzbekistan. It has even been suggested that a similar culture may have existed in Bactria, a possibility that seems to be confirmed by pottery from layer 6 at Mundigak, in southern Afghanistan.

The cultures of ancient Dakhistan and Yaz-depe I, therefore, show that the tribes of south-western Central Asia all developed along similar lines, characterized by the appearance of iron, the building of

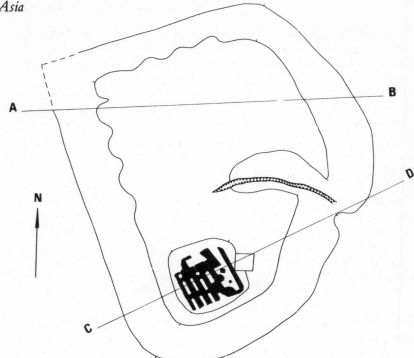

major irrigation systems and fortified citadels. In spite of the controversy over the question of the date of the rise of centralized states in Western Central Asia, it is clear that early in the first millennium BC the citadel of a large settlement would have kept the local rulers within its walls, separated from the mass of common people who lived in small dwellings at its foot. Indirect proof of the high level of social development is provided by the *Avesta*, which contains some data on the formation, in the ninth to seventh centuries BC, of an early class society in Western Central Asia, of the existence of slaves, and the building of canals. According to this source each region (*dakhyu*) was headed by a ruler (*dakhyupat*), and it even mentions a supreme ruler of all the regions (*dakhyupat* of all *dakhyu*), under whom there existed a 'council of first men'. This growing social differentiation was crystallized in the classic state organizations of Western Central Asia in the subsequent period.

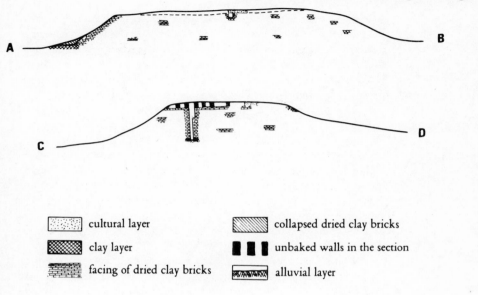

cultural layer		collapsed dried clay bricks	
clay layer		unbaked walls in the section	
facing of dried clay bricks		alluvial layer	

Fig. 46 Yaz-depe : plan (left) and enlarged sections of the citadel

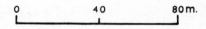

0   40   80 m.

It is clear that the Early Iron Age represents a second period of urban-ization, when fortified citadels once again rose up on the ruins of the abandoned settlements of the Late Bronze Age.

THE AMIRABAD CULTURE

In this respect the situation early in the first millennium BC on the northern edge of this region and particularly in Khorezm, is extremely interesting. The first few centuries of the first millennium BC saw the existence in this region of the Amirabad culture, represented by scattered sites, the most notable being Yakke Parsan. At this site were excavated two rows of more or less rectangular semi-subterranean dwellings, with storage pits and central hearths, divided by a street. The pottery was all hand-made, often burnished, and sometimes with incised decoration. Arti-facts of bronze include 'eyed' needles, awls, and arrow-heads. Of particular importance is the discovery of a bronze sickle, indicating that the people of Yakke Parsan were engaged in agriculture; the remains of a complex irrigation system in the form of canals running from the main stream of the Akcha Darya, on the banks of which stood the settlements of the Amirabad culture, confirms this. It is likely that this complex irrigation system originated from the local canals of the Bronze Age.

THE CHUST CULTURE

A similar situation existed in the Fergana Valley (Uzbekistan) in the late second and early first millennia BC, where what is known as the Chust culture has been identified. Although a great deal of material has been excavated, the origins of the Chust culture remain unclear, since there seems to be a long chronological gap between it and the local Neolithic cultures. It is probable, however, that the Chust culture arose as a result of the transition of the local tribes to farming under the in-fluence of those of southern Turkmenia.

The larger settlements of this culture seem to have covered more than 25 acres (Dalverzin, Ashkal-tepe), though others were smaller (Chust and Dekhkan). For the most part they consisted of semi-subterranean dwellings, although some houses were constructed on the surface, using sun-baked bricks. Some were fortified by defence walls, also of sun-baked brick. In addition to the normal graves, large numbers of dis-membered human bones and skulls were found in domestic pits, often together with animal bones and rubbish. Some of them show traces of burning, which may indicate 'head-hunting' or cannibalism.

Moulds for casting sickles and other implements have been found in these sites, pointing to a widespread use of metal artifacts in the Chust culture. Most of the objects were made of bronze; this, however, had a different chemical composition from the rest of the bronze in Western Central Asia, primarily because of the character of the local ore that was used. Among the implements were sickles, chisels, knives, awls, and needles; weapons included arrow-heads and spear-heads, and there was some horse harness equipment (bits). Jewellery, including bracelets, rings, and beads, was also found, and so were mirrors.

At the settlement of Dalverzin iron ore slag and an iron knife were found, indicating an acquaintance with this new metal. At the same time, stone was still widely used in the manufacture of querns, pounders, mortars, as well as hoes of massive proportions, knives, pin-heads, and casting moulds. Bone also played an important part, being used to make awls, bits, arrow-heads, and distaffs.

The pottery was hand-made, showing that the potter's wheel was still unknown in Fergana; that of the Chust culture was decorated with black paint on a red ground in geometric patterns of triangles and rhombs. This is very similar to the Yaz I pottery in southern Turkmenia, but it is difficult to draw any conclusions about a possible common root without more information about the huge territory adjoining the Fergana Valley and southern Turkmenia.

The Fergana Valley was a region with an established agricultural and stock-breeding economy, possibly even making use of artificial irri-gation. It was one of the centres of the ancient farming culture of Western Central Asia by the end of the second and beginning of the first millen-nium BC. We know very little yet about how early farming evolved in the Fergana Valley, but it seems certain that the pastoral-farming tribes of the steppes played a part in this process, Andronovo traditions being visible in the material culture.

Important qualitative changes took place at the beginning of the first millennium BC in Western Central Asia, not only in the traditionally agricultural regions in the south-west (southern Turkmenia), but also in areas where farming had been at a very primitive level (Khorezm), or perhaps totally unknown (Fergana). The cultural achievements of the agricultural oasis were diffused further and further northwards, into regions once populated by tribes of the Andronovo culture.

THE TAGISKEN CEMETERY

A striking example of the co-operation of the farming culture in the south of Western Central Asia and the steppe tribes of the north is the cemetery at Tagisken, in the delta of the Syr-Darya, in use from the tenth until the fifth century BC. Here, on the picturesque banks of the river, majestic tombs once rose, the largest of which, with a diameter of about 25 m., consisted of a cylindrical structure made of rectangular sun-baked bricks. Inside was a rectangular burial chamber, while the cylindrical structure itself was surrounded by a ring wall leaving a passage 2 m. wide between the two. The chamber contained over a hundred bronze nails which were apparently used to hold up the rugs that lined the walls.

Plate 52

Plate 53

In another type of tomb the outside wall of the structure was rec- tangular and the inner wall was circular, 14 m. in diameter. Within the inner wall brick columns formed a rectangle in the centre of which was the burial chamber. Around the tombs were groups of later burials surrounded by rectangular fences. Although all the tombs had been plundered and burned, the little that remained of the funerary offerings indicated the pomp and grandeur that must have marked the burial. These included some beautiful polished pottery with fine decoration, including a pottery vessel decorated with golden hoops, as well as weapons and jewellery of bronze and gold, which had either gone un- noticed or had been spurned by the robbers who looted all the more valuable items.

The cultural and historical interpretation of the cemetery is extremely difficult, but it is interesting to note that it contained hand-made, black, burnished pottery, hand-made pottery with incised decoration of late Andronovo type of southern Kazakhstan, as well as some pottery which was typical of the farming regions of south-west Central Asia. These factors led Tolstov to suggest that the Takisken cemetery was the burial ground of one of the most southerly Sachs tribes, the Sakaravaks, who were in contact with the agricultural population. This would explain not only the pottery but also the widespread use of sun-baked brick in the construction of tombs, which was not a building material normally favoured by nomads.

Tolstov was justified in comparing the Tagisken cemetery to the barrows of the Scythian kings, both on the strength of their size and the richness of the burial offerings. Only the leaders of the nomads (or perhaps they were kings by now) were able to have such elaborate tombs erected for their burial.

As may be judged from the evidence presented here, by the early first millennium BC in Western Central Asia there was a certain amount of social stratification not only in the traditionally farming population of the south, but also among the semi-nomadic tribes of the north. It was perhaps no accident that the Greek historian, Ctesias, refers to a Bactrian 'kingdom' which existed in Western Central Asia as far back as the eighth century BC, possibly a political union or a confederation of tribes, with which the Assyrian State had to reckon.

CHAPTER XI

Conclusion

Like the majority of peoples on this earth, the people of Western Central Asia have gone through two great epochs in their development—the food-collecting period and the food-production period. Food-collection (hunting, plant gathering and fishing) was the basis of the economy in the Palaeolithic Age, but with the improvement of implements, the accumulation of knowledge, and the slow but steady growth of the population, society was compelled to seek new ways of getting food; the most effective of these became the domestication of animals and the artificial cultivation of cereals.

With the shift to agriculture and stock-breeding as the basis of the economy, the rate of cultural development became increasingly disparate in the various regions of Western Central Asia. The material culture and highly productive agricultural economy of the Djeitun culture in South Central Asia stood in direct contrast to the cultures of the Caspian region, Kelteminar, Hissar, and Fergana, with their slow rate of progress in establishing the new type of economy. In the south of Western Central Asia, detailed research has provided evidence of the historical development of the agricultural communities. In the first period, as evidenced by for instance, the Neolithic culture of Djeitun, elements that characterized the food-collection economy and Mesolithic culture were still quite strong. In the subsequent period of maturity an agricultural and stock-breeding economy was fully established as seen in the relatively long Chalcolithic period, for example at Anau I-A, and Namazga I, II and III. The flowering of applied arts and particularly painted pottery is one of the indirect proofs of the high standard of living achieved by this society. This was succeeded by the advance from home production to specialized crafts by the introduction of the potter's wheel, kilns for the firing of ceramics, and the development of metallurgy, as well as an increased surplus production. In this period, exemplified by Namazga IV and V, the finest professional craftsmen were concentrated in large populated centres, where monumental buildings arose. That the budding urban civilization put paid to the primitive social order of equality is attested by the rich burials of the aristocracy and the priesthood.

Like the Harappan civilization and the Creto-Mycenaean kingdoms, the culture of Altin-depe eventually fell into a decline and the entire community seems to have regressed to the beginning of the period of craft specialization. Meanwhile, the rest of Western Central Asia was gradually catching up with the achievements of southern Turkmenia. Throughout the second millennium BC, the Steppe Bronze Age tribes of Western Central Asia were developing the interfluvial area, choosing favourable spots to found their agricultural oases. During the first millennium BC the unequal rates of development became less marked, as the agricultural settlements of the Chust culture flourished in Fergana, and intensive irrigation farming developed in the lower reaches of the Amu-Darya. The decline of south Turkmenian culture was arrested and once again fortified proto-urban centres arose. Thus Western Central Asian civilization, which had been born on the edge of the Kara-Kum desert, gradually became a civilization based on large rivers, including the valleys of the Murgab, the Zeravshan, and the Amu-Darya.

In each of these periods, the relationship of the population of Western Central Asia with various neighbouring nations and tribes was different. During the Lower Palaeolithic Age, Western Central Asia lay midway between two cultural worlds—the western world with its 'classic' types of implements and the eastern world with its pebble-tool industries. Gradually connections with the Near East predominated and these became the most progressive and decisive, no doubt exerting a powerful influence on the early development of agriculture and on the Djeitun culture in the south of Western Central Asia, which was in fact a northern outpost of the Near Eastern world. Mesopotamian contacts, often associated it seems with the direct movement of peoples, were clearly felt throughout the Chalcolithic period. These contacts, in which the Western Central Asian tribes took part, eventually extended to southern Afghanistan and Baluchistan. Meanwhile in the north of Western Central Asia, the Kelteminar culture with its archaic cultural features brought a large part of Asia into the Neolithic world and acted as a unique kind of advanced centre and transmitter of cultural developments.

In the period of budding urban civilization, the traditional Meso-potamian-Iranian contacts were supplemented by strong ties with ancient Indian Harappa. The troubled times which marked the decline of this first Western Central Asian civilization and the spread of the Steppe Bronze Age tribes were probably associated with the complex process of the migration of peoples belonging to the Indo-Iranian language group, in which many of the modern peoples of Western Central Asia, Afghanistan, Iran, and India had their origins. Thus all the evidence clearly reveals the close and indissoluble links between the history of Western Central Asia and that of its neighbours. Close ties and mutual influence have from the earliest times lighted the difficult road of the progress of mankind.

Notes on the Text

CHAPTER II

1 On the correlation of the Quaternary period in Western Central Asia with the transgressions of the Caspian Sea, see: N. N. Kostenko, G. F. Tetiukhin, and P. V. Fedorov, *BKICP*, No. 27, 1962. On the geographical allocation of Palaeolithic sites, see: V. A. Ranov, *Osnovniye problemi izucheniya chetvertichnogo perioda,* Moscow, 1965.

2 For instance, near Kasir Bulak on the Krasnovodsk peninsular (A. P. Okladnikov, Early Prehistoric Sites of the Krasnovodsk Peninsular, *TYuTAKE* II, Ashkhabad 1953); in the Kopet Dag mountains. (B. K. Luzgin and V. A. Ranov. The First Discoveries of the Palaeolithic in the Central Kopet Dag mountains, *BKICP* 32, 1966); in southern Fergana (A. P. Okladnikov and N. I. Leonov, The First Discoveries of the Stone Age in Fergana, *KSIA* 82, 1961; M. P. Kasymov, Research on the Palaeolithic of the Fergana Valley in 1964, *Istoriya material'noi kul'tury Uzbekistana,* 7, Tashkent, 1966); and in the uplands of western Tadjikistan (A. P. Okladnikov, Stone Age Sites in Tadjikistan, *MIA,* 66, 1958; V. A. Ranov, *The Stone Age of Tadjikistan,* Dushanbe, 1962.)

3 D. N. Lev thinks that there is a possible connection between the Samarkand campsite and the sites in Siberia, while V. A. Ranov connects it with the 'Asiatic' line of development of Palaeolithic sites in Central Asia, possibly in association with traditions of the pebble-tool cultures. A. P. Okladnikov,

however, rightly points out the absence at the Samarkand campsite of scrapers characteristic of the Upper Palaeolithic sites in Siberia. This is most probably an assemblage of a rather unusual local Central Asian industry of 'non-Aurignacian' type.

CHAPTER III

1 The most detailed results of excavations to be published have been those carried out at the Djebel Cave (A. P. Okladnikov, Djebel Cave, an Early Prehistoric Site on the Caspian Shores of Turkmenia, *TYuTAKE*, VII, 1956; and Stone Age Sites in Turkmenia, *Izv. AN Turkm. SSR,* 2, 1953; G. E. Markov, Dam-Dam-Chashma Cave no. 2 on the Eastern Shores of the Caspian, *SA,* 2, 1956).

2 It is interesting to note that geometric implements, which were so numerous in Zarzi and Palegawra, almost completely disappeared in northern Iran but returned in great abundance in the Jarmo period.

3 The Djeitun material is closest to layers 5 and 5a of the Djebel cave, and to layer 3 of the Dam-Dam-Chashma cave 2. We do not share the opinion of G. A. Markov, that Djeitun was synchronous with layer 4 (upper).

4 This date is based on the synchronization of layer 3 at Dam-Dam-Chashma with Djeitun, which was dated to the sixth millennium BC.

5 Korobkova and Ranov suggest that this assemblage should be dated to the ninth/tenth millennia BC. The upper part of

horizon II has a carbon 14 date of 5150±
140 BC.

6 The Obi-Shir I and Obi-Shir II caves were
excavated by U. Islamov, the Tash-Kumir
cave by M. B. Yunusaliyev.

7 *Radiocarbon*, vol. 9, 1967, p. 360.

8 In northern Afghanistan bones of domesticated sheep and goat were discovered in the
Gari-Mar cave in layers which are dated to
the sixth millennium BC. (S. Dupree, The
Prehistoric Period of Afghanistan, *Afghanistan*, 3, 1967, p. 24.)

CHAPTER IV

1 Originally, only two phases of the Djeitun
culture were distinguished (V. M. Masson,
Djeitun Culture, *TYuTAKE*, X, 1961),
but the discovery of new sites has since indicated a third phase (O. K. Berdyiev,
southern Turkmenia in the Neolithic Period,
Avtoreferativnaya dissertatsiya, Ashkhabad,
1965).

2 The most realistic estimate of the duration
of a pisé dwelling, if regularly repaired, is
50–60 years (R. Ghirshman, *Fouilles de
Sialk*, vol. I, Paris, 1938, p. 89).

3 The 'standard painted pottery' which occurs
in Tepe Guran shows close similarities to
Djeitun (J. Meldgaard, P. Mortensen, H.
Thranc, Excavations at Tepe Guran, Lur-
istan, *Acta Archaeologia*, XXXIV, 1963).
Pottery painted in the Sorab style may have
had an influence on the westernmost site of
the Djeitun culture in south Turkmenistan
—the village of Bami (O. K. Berdyiev,
The Stratigraphy of the Settlement of Bami,
SA 4, 1963, figs, 3, 18; 4, 7).

4 This explanation was given by S. A.
Semenov and G. F. Korobkova. *Cf.* a clay
board with similar counters in Egypt.

CHAPTER V

1 Mural frescoes were discovered on the
northern mound at Anau during excavations in 1953 (S. A. Yershov, The Northern
Mound at Anau, *TIIAE AN TSSR*, II,
1956). The frescoes at the settlement of
Yassi-depe were discovered by B. A. Kuftin:
Research into the Anau Culture by the
South Turkmenian Archaeological Expedition in 1952, *IAN TSSR*, I, 1954.

2 It is important to note, in the earliest period
of the Kelteminar culture, the similarity
between the sickle blades from the Tuz-
kanian sites and similar blades from the Late
Djeitun sites.

CHAPTER VI

1 The well-known rivalry between Sumer
and Elam and the forced founding of an
Elamite trading station on the ruins of Sialk
III give certain basic grounds for such an
assumption.

CHAPTER VII

1 An indication of cultural contacts with
neighbouring tribes may be seen in a
painted vessel from Muhammedabad (Iran),
which was possibly imported from Namazga-depe, only 30 km. away (H. Frankfort,
Studies in the Early Pottery of the Near East,
vol. 1; A. Ya. Shchetenko, Bronze Age
Painted Pottery from Namazga-depe, *KSIA*,
vol. 98, 1964, fig. 20).

CHAPTER VIII

1 The profoundly specific 'national' character of the culture of Harappa and China of
the Shang period seems to indicate very
definitely that urbanization in these regions
took place independently.

2 On the basis of the first attempt at recon-struction, which was made after the 1967 season, and published in *Antiquity*, it was assumed that there was a hearth-altar at the top of the tower platform. In the light of the 1968 excavations, however, this inter-pretation seems to be incorrect.

3 Such vessels were often met with in child-ren's burials and may indeed have been milk-jugs.

4 This is indicated by the finds of seals at a number of sites on the Persian Gulf and at Harappan trade colonies (G. F. Dales, Harappan Outposts on the Makran Coast, *Antiquity*, XXXVI, 1962, 86–92).

5 In Sumer, the goddess of corn was Ashnan, while Nanshe was connected with water. The material from Sumer serves as an ex-cellent illustration of the great role played by local divinities, and the local pantheons that were formed around them, the goddess of fertility generally being in the centre (this was Inanna in Uruk, Bou or Babu in Lagash, Ninkhursag in Eredu). It may be that figurines with the symbol of the tri-angle with cilia, found only at Altin-depe, represent the local fertility goddess, patroness of this second capital of southern Turk-menia.

6 Such comparisons do not, of course, mean that we must 'read' our symbols on the basis of Sumerian or proto-Elamite writing, especially since there is also a definite chronological gap. On the other hand, the proto-Elamite pictographs do survive into the second half of the third millennium BC, and could have exerted an indirect influence on the oases of southern Turkmenistan (through Sialk?).

CHAPTER IX

1 Excavated by A. Ya. Shchetenko in 1968. Previously it had been thought, on the basis of the work of B. A. Kuftin in 1952, that the total thickness of the layers was 7 m., but after the excavations of 1965–68 at Altin-depe it became possible to relate to the Namazga V culture the earlier stages of pottery previously described as Namazga IV ware.

2 In recent years this problem has been most thoroughly studied by V. S. Sorokin, using the material of the Andronovo culture as a basis (V. S. Sorokin, A Bronze Age Cemetery at Tasti-butak I, in western Kazakhstan, *MIA* 120, Moscow-Lenin-grad, 1962).

3 The new discoveries, however, seem to have led to an over-estimation of the importance of agriculture in the complex economy of the Tazabagiab tribes of Khorezm. It should not be forgotten that stable, settled villages came into being here much later.

4 B. A. Litvinski seems to relate all Central Asian sites of the Andronovo type to the Kairak-Kum culture except those in the lower Amu-Darya. But as we see from a more detailed analysis, the sites of the Zeravshan and the Tashkent Oasis differ noticeably from the Kairak-Kum com-plexes proper.

5 A settlement of this new culture was dis-covered by L. I. Albaum near Termez.

6 In the lower reaches of the Amu-Darya, its foundation, according to S. P. Tolstov, may have been the Late Kelteminar culture (S. P. Tolstov, *Traces of the Civilization of Ancient Khorezm*, Moscow, 1948, p. 76). In western Tadjikistan a similar part was played by the Late Hissar element (B. A.

Litvinski, V. A. Ranov, Excavations at the shelter of An-Tangi in 1959, *TIIAE AN TSSR*, 31, 1961). B. A. Latynin, however, suggests that the Zaman-baba culture had its roots in the Andronovo culture.

7 The assemblages identified by S. P. Tolstov and his pupils as belonging to a specific Suyargan culture can probably be considered as an example of this.

8 It is interesting to note that at the An-dronovo cemetery of Tasti-Butak, the An-dronovo physical anthropological type,

which was characteristic of man in central and eastern Kazakhstan and southern Sib-eria, is totally absent. (K. V. Sal'nikov, *The Ancient History of the Southern Urals*, Moscow, 1967, pp. 344-47).

9 This also applies to the two kinds of hearth-altars, the fire and solar symbols, the wheel and the swastika, as well as the rite of cremation and other elements.

CHAPTER X

1 The iron sickle from the southern mound at Anau dates to this period.

Bibliography

ABBREVIATIONS

BKICP	Biuleten Komissi po Izucheniya Chetvertnogo Perioda
IAN TSSR	Izvestiya Akademii Nauk Turkmenskoi SSR
KSIA	Kratkiye Soobshcheniya Instituta Arkheologii
KSIIMK	Kratkiye Soobshcheniya Instituta Istorii Materialy Kultury, Moscow
MASI	Memoires of the Archae-ological Survey of India, Calcutta
MDAFA	Mémoires de la Délégation archaeologique Francaise en Afghanistan
MDP	Mémoires de la Délégation en Perse, Paris
MIA	Materiale i Issledovanii po Arkheologii, Moscow

OIP	Oriental Institute of Chicago Publications
SA	Sovyetskaya Arkheologiya, Moscow
SAOC	Studies in Ancient Oriental Civilization, Chicago University
Sbornik MAE	Sbornik Muzeja Arkheologii i Etnografi, Leningrad
SE	Sovyetskaya Etnografia
TIIAE AN TSSR	Trudy Instituta Istorii, Arkheologii i Etnografii Akademii Nauk Tadzhikstan SSR
TYuTAKE	Trudy Yuzhno-Turk-menistanskoi Arkheolo-gicheskoi Komplexnoi Expeditsii, Ashkabad
VDI	Vyestnik Drevnei Istorii, Leningrad

Entries marked with an asterisk are in English; other titles have been translated.

GENERAL

ATAGARRYIEV, E. and BERDYIEV, O. Archaeological research in Turkmenistan during the period of Soviet government, *SA*, 3, 1967.

*CHILDE, G. The Urban Revolution, *Town Planning Review*, XXI, 1950, i.

*— New Light on the Most Ancient East, London, 1952.

*COON, C. S. *Cave Explorations in Iran, 1949*, Philadelphia, 1951.

*— The Seven Caves, New York, 1957.

*COON, C. S. and RALPH, K. Radiocarbon Dates for Kara-Kamar, Afghanistan, *Science*, vol. 122, 1955.

*DYSON, R. Problems in the Relative Chronology of Iran, in: *Chronologies in Old World Archaeology*, ed. R. EHRICH, Chicago, 1965.

*LLOYD, S. *The Art of the Ancient Near East*, London, 1961

KOROBKOVA, G. F., KRIZHEVSKAYA, L. YA., and MANDEL'SHTAM, A. M. *The History, Archaeology and Ethnography of Central Asia*, Moscow, 1968.

MASSON, V. M. *Central Asia and the Near East*, Moscow-Leningrad, 1964.

*— The Urban Revolution in South Turkmenia, *Antiquity* XLII, 1968, 178–87

MASSON, V. M. and SARIANIDI, V. I. *Seven Goddesses of the Early Agriculturalists*, Moscow, 1969

*MCCOWN, D. The Comparative Stratigraphy of Early Iran, *SAOC*, 23, Chicago, 1941.

OKLADNIKOV, A. P. The Early Prehistory of Turkmenistan, *TIIAE AN TSSR*, 1, Ashkhabad, 1956.

— Central Asia in the Stone and Bronze Ages (ed.), Moscow-Leningrad, 1966.

*PIGGOT, S. *Prehistoric India*, London, 1962.

SCHAEFFER, C. *Stratigraphie Comparée et Chronologie de l'Asie Occidentale*, Oxford, 1948.

*SCHMIDT, H. Archaeological Excavations in Anau and Old Merv, in: PUMPELLY, R. *Explorations in Turkestan*, vol. 1, Washington, 1908.

CHAPTER II

ALPYSBAIEV, KH. Discoveries of Early and Late Palaeolithic Sites in southern Kazakhstan, *SA*, No. 1, 1961.

BIBIKOVA, V. I. Remarks on the Fauna of the Mousterian Cave of Aman Kutan I, *SA*, No. 3, 1958.

BORDES, F. *Typologie du Paleolithique Ancien et Moyen*, Bordeaux, 1961.

BUNAK V. V. The Impression of the Braincase in the Palaeolithic Child's Skull from Teshik-Tash Cave, Uzbekistan, *Sbornik MAE*, t. XIII, 1951.

KASYMOV, M. P. Chipped Stone Manufacture of the Stone Age in Central Asia, *Avtoreferativnaya dissertatsiya*, Leningrad, 1962.

KASYMOV, M. R. The Stratified Palaeolithic Site of Kul Bulak, *Problemy arkheologii Srednei Azii*, Leningrad, 1962.

LEV, D. N. The Lower Palaeolithic in Aman Kutan, *Trudy Uzbekskogo Gosudarstvennego Universiteta, nov. ser.*, v. 61, Samarkand, 1956.

— The Palaeolithic Settlement in Samarkand, *Trudy Samarkandskogo Gosudarstvennego Universiteta*, v. 135, Samarkand, 1964.

— The Samarkand Palaeolithic Site, *Istoriya material'noi kul'tury Uzbekistana*, v. 6, Tashkent, 1965.

LITVINSKI, B. A., OKLADNIKOV, A. P., RANOV, V. A., *The Ancient Past of Kairak-Kum*, Dushanbe, 1962.

MEDOYEV, A. G. A Manufacturing Site at Lake Kudaikol, *Novoye v arkheologii Kazakhstana*, Alma-Ata, 1968.

*MOVIUS, H. L. *Early Man and Pleistocene Stratigraphy, Southern and Eastern Asia,* Cambridge, Mass., 1944.

*— *The Mousterian Cave of Teshik-Tash,* Cambridge, Mass., 1953.

NASRETDINOV, KH. K. Khodjakent cave, no. 2—a Mousterian site near Tashkent, *Obshchestvennyie nauki v Uzbekistane*, No. 4, 1962.

— Obi-Rakhmat cave, *Istoriya material'noi kul'tury Uzbekistana*, v. 5. Tashkent, 1964.

OKLADNIKOV, A. P. Amir Temir—a New Stone Age site in the Baisuntan Mountains (Uzbekistan). *KSIIMK*, v. 6, 1940.

— *Palaeolithic Man*, Moscow, 1949.

— Khodjakent Cave—a New Mousterian Site in Uzbekistan, *KSIA*, v. 82, 1961.

RANOV, V. A. Local Palaeolithic Cultures in Central Asia, *Izvestia Otdeleniya Obshchestvennykh Nauk Akademii Nauk Tadzhikskoi SSR*, v. 3 (53), Dushanbe, 1968.

SULEIMANOV, R. KH. The Development of a Local Stone Industry, *Istoriya materiyal'noi kul'tury Uzbekistana*, v. 7, Tashkent, 1966.

— Obi-Rakhmat Cave and a statistical Study of the Obi-Rakhmat Culture, *Avtoreferativnaya dissertatsiya*, Tashkent, 1968.

CHAPTER III

FORMOZOV, A. A. The Rock Paintings of Zaraut-Kamar in the Gorge of the Zaraut-sai, *SA*, No. 4, 1966.

KOROBKOVA, G. F. The Mesolithic and Neolithic Cultures of Central Asia, *Problems in the Archaeology of Western Central Asia*, Leningrad, 1968.

MASSON, V. M. The Mesolithic of the Near East, *MIA*, No. 126, Moscow-Leningrad, 1966.

RANOV, V. A. Stone Age Engravings in the Shakhta Cave, *SE*, No. 6, 1961.

CHAPTER IV

BERDYIEV, O. K. Chagilli-depe—a New Site of the Neolithic Djeitun Culture, *Material'naya kul'tura narodov Srednei Azii i Kazakhstana*, Moscow, 1966.

— A Study of Neolithic Sites (in Central Asia), *Karakumskiye drevnosti*, I, Ashkhabad, 1968.

*CRAWFORD, V. E. Beside the Kara Su, (Yarim Tepe excavations), *Bulletin, The Metropolitan Museum of Art*, April, 1963.

*HARLAN, Y. R. A Wild Wheat Harvest in Turkey, *Archaeology*, 1967.

KOROBKOVA, G. F. The Determination of the Function of Stone and Bone Implements at the Djeitun Site on the Basis of Working Traces, *TYuTAKE*, t. X, Ashkhabad, 1961.

— The Production Tools from the Settlements of Chopan-depe, Togolok-depe and Pessedjik-depe, *Karakumskiye drevnosti*, I, Ashkhabad, 1968.

— Tools and Implements of the Neolithic Communities of Central Asia, *MIA* 158, 1970.

KOROBKOVA, G. F., KRIZHEVSKAYA, L., MANDEL'SHTAM, A. The Neolithic of the East Coast of the Caspian Sea, *The History, Archaeology and Ethnography of Central Asia*, Moscow-Leningrad, 1968.

KOROBKOVA, G. F., RANOV, V. A. The Neolithic of the Mountain Regions of Central

Asia, *Problemy arkheologii Srednei Azii,* Leningrad, 1968.

MARKOV, G. E. The Dam-Dam-Chashma 2 cave on the East Coast of the Caspian, *SA,* No. 2, 1966.

*MASSON, V. M. The Neolithic Farmers of Central Asia, *Antiquity,* 1965.

— The Evolution of Defence Walls in Sedentary Settlements, *KSIA,* No. 108, Moscow, 1966.

*MORTENSEN, P. Additional Remarks on the Chronology of Early Village-Farming Communities in the Zagros Area, *Sumer,* v. XX, 1964.

OKLADNIKOV, A. P. Djebel cave: a Prehistoric Site on the Caspian Shores of Turkmenia, *TYuTAKE,* t. VII, Ashkhabad, 1956.

— Stone Age Investigations in Tadjikistan in 1957, *TIIAE AN TSSR,* C III, Dushanbe, 1959.

VINOGRADOV, A. V. *Neolithic sites of Khorezm,* Moscow, 1968.

— The Neolithic of Kizil-Kum (Kelteminar Culture), *Problemy arkheologii Srednei Azii,* Leningrad, 1968.

ZADNEPROVSKY, YU. A. The Neolithic of Central Fergana, *KSIA,* v. 108, Moscow, 1966.

CHAPTER V

BERDYIEV, O. Chakmakli-depe—a New Site from the Anau I-A Period, *Istoriya, arkheologiya i etnografiya Srednei Azii,* Moscow, 1968.

*CALDWELL, I. *Investigations at Tal-i-Iblis,* Chicago, 1967.

CHERNYKH, E. N. A Study of the Metal of the Anau culture, *KSIA,* v. 91, 1962.

GANIALIN, A. F. The mound of Ilginli-depe,

TIIAE AN TSSR, t. 5, 1959.

— Altin-depe (the 1953 excavations), *TIIAE AN TSSR,* t. 5, 1959.

GULIAMOV, YA. G., ISLAMOV, U., ASKAROV, A. *Prehistoric Culture and the Rise of Irrigation Agriculture in the Lower Reaches of the Zeravshan.*

KHLOPIN, I. N. Dashlidji-depe and the Chalcolithic Farmers of southern Turkmenistan, *TYuTAKE,* t. X, 1960.

— Sites of the early Chalcolithic in southern Turkmenia, Moscow-Leningrad, 1963.

— The Geoksyur Group of Settlements in the Chalcolithic Period, Moscow-Leningrad, 1964.

LISITSINA, G. N. Irrigation Agriculture in the Chalcolithic Period in southern Turkmenia, *MIA,* No. 128, Moscow, 1965.

LISITSINA, G. N., MASSON, V. M., SARIANIDI, V. I., KHLOPIN, I. N. An Archaeological and Palaeo-geographical Study of the Geoksyur oasis, *SA,* No. 1, 1965.

MASSON, V. M. Kara-depe near Artyk, *TYuTAKE,* t. X, 1960.

— The south Turkmenian Centre of Early Agriculturalists, *TYuTAKE,* t. X, Ashkhabad, 1960.

— Eastern Parallels of the Ubaid Culture, *KSIA,* v. 91, 1962.

— Middle Chalcolithic Sites of South West Turkmenia, Moscow, 1962.

MARKOV, G. E. Excavations of the prehistoric site of Ojukli, *Vestnik Moskovskogo Universiteta, seriya 9,* No. 3, 1961.

SARIANIDI, V. I. The Stratigraphy of the Eastern Group of Sites of the Anau Culture, *SA,* No. 3, 1960.

— The Early Architecture of the Chalcolithic Settlements of the Geoksyur Oasis, *KSIA,* v. 91, 1962.

— The Secret of the Vanished Art of the Kara Kum, Moscow, 1967.

VINOGRADOV, A. V. The Southern Connections of the Kelteminar Culture, SE, No. 1, 1957.

CHAPTER VI

CASAL, J. M. Fouilles de Mundigak, MDAFA, t. XVII, Paris, 1961.

*DALES, G. A Suggested Chronology for Afghanistan, Baluchistan and the Indus Valley, Chronologies in Old World Archaeology, ed. R. Ehrich, 1965.

*CARDI, B. DE Excavations and Reconaissance in Kalat, West Pakistan, Pakistan Archaeology, 2, Karachi, 1965.

*FAIRSERVIS, W. The Origin, Character and Decline of an Early Civilization, Museum Novitates, 2302, 1967.

GAUTIER, G., LAMPZE, G. Fouilles de Mussian, MDP, t. VIII, Paris, 1905.

*HERZFELD, E. Iran in the Ancient East, London-New York, 1941.

KHLOPIN, I. N. The Ethnic Characteristics of the Early Farmers of Southern Turkmenia, SE, No. 5, 1960.

*LANGSDORF, A., MCCOWN, D. Tell-i-Bakun, Philadelphia, 1937.

*LE BRETON, L. The Early Periods at Susa, Mesopotamian Relations, Iraq, XIX, 1957.

*MALLOWAN, M. Excavations at Tall Chagar Basar and Archaeological Survey of the Habur Region, Iraq, III, London, 1936.

MASSON, V. M. Painted Pottery Excavated by B. A. Kuftin in South Turkmenia, TYuTAKE, t. VII, 1956.

— Kara-depe near Artyk, TYuTAKE, t. X, 1960.

— Middle Chalcolithic Sites of S. W. Turkmenia, Moscow-Leningrad, 1962.

— Eastern Parallels of the Ubaid Culture, KSIA, v. 91, 1962.

— The Tradition of Collective Burial in the Chalcolithic Period of Central Asia, Afghanistan and India, KSIA, v. 101, 1964.

— Review of the book by J. M. Casal, Fouilles de Mundigak, SA, 4, 1964.

*OATES, J. First Preliminary Report on a Survey in the Region of Mandali and Badra, Sumer, t. XXII, 1966, Baghdad.

*PERKINS, A. The Comparative Archaeology of Early Mesopotamia, SAOC, 25, Chicago, 1957.

SARIANIDI, V. I. The Chalcolithic Settlement of Geoksyur, TYuTAKE, t. X, 1960.

— The Stratigraphy of the Eastern Group of Sites of the Anau Culture, SA, No. 3, 1960.

— Ritual Buildings of the Settlements of the Anau Culture, SA, No. 1, 1962.

— Late Chalcolithic Sites of S. E. Turkmenia, Moscow, 1965.

— Review of Pakistan Archaeology, 2; SA, 1, 1969.

*SCHMIDT, E. Excavations at Tepe Hissar, Philadelphia, 1937.

*STEIN, A. Archaeological Reconnaissance in North-Western India and South-Eastern Iran, London, 1937.

*TOBLER, A. Excavations at Tepe Gawra, II, 1950.

TROFIMOVA, T. A., GINSBURG, V. V. The Physical Anthropological Composition of the Chalcolithic Population of S. Turkmenia, TYuTAKE, t. X, 1960.

CHAPTER VII

*ARNE, T. J. Excavations at Shah tepe, Stockholm, 1945.

BRAIDWOOD, R., BRAIDWOOD, L. Excavations in the Plain of Antioch, Chicago, 1960.

GANIALIN, A. F. Archaeological Sites in the Mountainous Regions of the North-West Kopet Dag, *IAN TSSR*, No. 5, 1953.

— The 1959–1961 Excavations at Altin-depe, *SA*, No. 4, 1967.

MASSON, V. M. Proto-urban Civilization in the South of Soviet Central Asia, *SA*, No. 3, 1967.

SARIANIDI, V. I. Pottery Manufacture in the Settlements of Ancient Margiana, *TYu-TAKE*, t. VIII, 1958.

— Khapuz-depe, a Bronze Age Site, *KSIA*, v. 98, 1964.

— Excavations of the Mounds of Geoksyur and Altin-depe, *Arkheologicheskiye otkrytiya 1965 goda*, Moscow, 1966.

— Excavations at Khapuz-depe and Altin-depe, *Arkheologicheskiye otkrytiya 1966 goda*, Moscow, 1967.

— Further Investigations at Ulug-depe, *Arkheologicheskiye otkrytiye 1968 goda*, Moscow, 1969.

— Southern Turkmenia and Northern Iran: Early cremations and differences, *SA*, No. 3, 1969.

SHCHETENKO, A. YA. Excavations of Chalcolithic and Bronze Age Sites in the Kaakhkin Region, *Karakumskiye drevnosti*, v. I, 1968.

WULSIN, F. R. Excavations at Tureng Tepe, Supplement to Bulletin of American Institute for Persian Art and Archaeology, v. 2, 1932.

VAN BUREN Clay Figurines of Babylonia and Assyria, Chicago, 1940.

CHAPTER VIII

FAIRSERVIS, W. A. Archaeological Studies in the Seistan Basin of South-Western Afghanistan and Eastern Iran, New York, 1961.

GULIAMOV, YA. G., ISLAMOV, U., ASKAROV, A. *Prehistoric Culture and the Use of Irrigation Agriculture in the Lower Reaches of the Zeravshan*, Tashkent, 1966.

KUZ'MINA, E. E. *Chalcolithic and Bronze Age Metal Artifacts in Central Asia*, Moscow, 1966.

— The Cemetery of Zaman-baba, *SE*, No. 2, 1958.

LISITSINA, G. N. Earliest Irrigation in Turkmenia, Antiquity XLIII, 1969, 279–88.

LITVINSKI, B. A. Namazga-depe, *SE*, No. 4, 1952.

MASSON, V. M. The Early Agricultural Culture of Margiana, *MIA*, No. 73, Moscow-Leningrad, 1959.

— The Discovery of Bronze Age Monumental Architecture in S. Turkmenia, *SA*, No. 2, 1968.

— The Fourth Season of Excavations at Altin-depe, *Arkheologicheskiye otkrytiya 1968 goda*, Moscow, 1969.

MASSON, V. M., SARIANIDI, V. I. The Symbols on the Central Asian Bronze Age Figurines, *VDI*, No. 1, 1969.

NORMAN BROWN, W. The Indian Games of Pachis, Chaupur and Chausar, Expedition, No. 3, 1964.

SARIANIDI, V. I. Pottery Manufacture in the Settlements of Ancient Margiana, *TYu-TAKE*, t. VIII, Ashkhabad, 1958.

SHCHETENKO, A. YA. Southern Turkmenian Parallels of the Harappan Culture, *Problemy arkheologii Srednei Azii*, Leningrad, 1968.

— Excavations of Chalcolithic and Bronze Age Sites in the Kaakhkin Region, *Karakumskiye drevnosti*, v. I, 1968.

— Taichanak-depe, *Karakumskiye drevnosti*,

v. 2, Ashkhabad, 1969.

*SCHMIDT, E. *Excavations at Tepe Hissar,* Philadelphia, 1937.

SOROKIN, S. S. The Hoard from Khaka, *Soobscheniya Gosudarstvennogo Ermitazha,* v. 19, 1960.

YERMOLOVA, N. M. Mammal Bone Remains from the Chalcolithic and Bronze Age Sites of Southern Turkmenia, *Karakum-skiye drevnosti,* v. 1, Ashkhabad, 1968.

CHAPTER IX

ABETEKOV, A. Bronze Age Burials in the Cemetery of Tegirmen-sai, *KSIA,* v. 93, Moscow, 1963.

AKISHEV, K. A., KUSHAYEV, G. A. *The Culture of the Ancient Saki and Usuni in the Valley of the Il,* Alma-Ata, 1963.

ASKAROV, A. Sites of the Andronovo Culture in the Lower Basin of the Zeravshan, *Istoriya material'noi kul'tury Uzbekistana,* v. 3, Tashkent, 1962.

BERNSHTAM, A. H. Historico-archaeological observations of the Central Tien-Shen and the Pamiro-Alaia, *MIA,* No. 26, Moscow-Leningrad, 1952.

D'YAKONOV, P. M. *The History of the Medes,* Moscow-Leningrad, 1956.

GAMBURG, B. Z., GORBUNOVA, N. G. A Bronze Age Cemetery in the Fergana Valley, *KSIIMK,* v. 63, Moscow, 1956.

GANIALIN, A. F. Bronze Age Graves at the Village of Yangi-kala, *TYuTAKE,* t. VII, Ashkhabad, 1956.

— Tekkem-depe, *TIIAE AN TSSR,* t. II, Ashkhabad, 1956.

GINSBURG, V. V. The Physical Anthropology of the Late Bronze Age Population of Southern Turkmenia, *TYuTAKE,* t. IX, Ashkhabad, 1959.

GRIAZNOV, M. P. The Steppe Pastoralists of Central Asia in the Middle and Late Bronze Age, *Problemy arkheologii Srednei Azii,* Leningrad, 1968.

GULIAMOV, YA. G., ISLAMOV, U., ASKAROV, A. *Prehistoric Culture and the Rise of Irrigation Agriculture in the Lower Reaches of the Zeravshan,* Tashkent, 1966.

ITINA, M. A. Excavations of a Cemetery of the Tazabagiab Culture at Kokcha 3, *Materialy Khorezmskoi Ekspeditsii,* v. 5, Moscow, 1961.

— The Farmers of Ancient Khorezm, *Istoria arkheologiia i etnografiya Srednei Azii,* Moscow-Leningrad, 1968.

KHLOPIN, I. N. The 'Tower' of Namazga-depe, *Arkheologicheskiye otkrytiya 1965 goda,* Moscow, 1966.

— Excavations at Namazga-depe, *Arkheologicheskiye otkrytiya 1967 goda,* Moscow 1968.

KOZHEMIAKO, P. N. Bronze Age Burials in Khirgizia, *Izvestia AN Kirg. SSR, Ser. obshch, nauk,* t. II, No. 3. Frunze, 1960.

KUZ'MINA, E. E. *Chalcolithic and Bronze Age Metal Artifacts in Central Asia,* Moscow, 1966.

LATYNIN, B. A. The Southern Boundaries of the *Oikmene* of the Steppe Bronze Age Cultures, *SA,* No. 3, 1958.

MANDEL'SHTAM, A. M. Timber Graves in Southern Turkmenia, *KSIA,* v. 108, Moscow, 1966.

— New Timber Graves in Southern Turkmenia, *KSIA,* v. 112, Moscow, 1967.

— Bronze Age Sites in Southern Turkmenistan, *MIA,* No. 145, Moscow-Leningrad, 1968.

MASSON, V. M. The Early Agricultural Culture of Margiana, *MIA,* No. 73, Moscow-

Leningrad, 1959.

SMIRNOV, K. F. The Origin of the Early Sarmatians, *SA*, No. 3, 1957.

TOLSTOV, S. P. Ancient Khorezm Sites in Kara-Kalpaki, *VDI*, No. 3, 1939.

TROFIMOVA, T. A. *The Ancient Population of Khorezm on the Basis of Palaeoanthropological Investigations*, Moscow, 1959.

CHAPTER X

BOGDANOVA-BEREZOVSKAYA, I. V. The Chemical Composition of the Metal Artifacts from Fergana in the Bronze and Iron Ages, *MIA*, No. 118, Moscow-Leningrad, 1962.

GANIALIN, A. F. Archaeological Sites of the Mountain Regions of the North-west Kopet Dag, *IAN TSSR*, No. 5, 1953.

*HERSHEVITCH, I. *Avestian Hymn to Muthra*, Cambridge, 1959.

ITINA, M. A. The Settlement of Yakke-Parsan 2, *Sbornik Materialy Khorezmkoi Ekspeditsii*, v. 6, 1963.

KACHURIS, K. A. Excavations at Elken-depe in Southern Turkmenia, *Arkheologicheskiye otkrytiya 1966 goda*, Moscow, 1967.

MARUSHCHENKO, A. A. Elken-depe, *TIIAE AN TSSR*, t.v., 1959.

MASSON, V. M. Sites of the Culture of Ancient Dagistan in South-west Turkmenia, *TYu-TAKE*, t. VII, 1956.

— Painted Pottery from the Excavations of B. A. Kuftin in Southern Turkmenia, *TYuTAKE*, t. VII, 1956.

— The Early Agricultural Culture of Margiana, *MIA*, No. 73, 1959.

SARIANIDI, V. I. Further Investigations at Ulug-depe, *Arkheologicheskiye otkrytiya 1968 goda*, Moscow, 1969.

SPRISHEVSKII, V. I. The Settlement of Chust, *Avtoreferativnaya dissertatsiya*, 1963.

TOLSTOV, S. P., ITINA, M. A. The Problem of the Suyargan Culture, *SA*, No. 1, 1960.

TOLSTOV, S. P. *At the Ancient Delta of the Oxus and Yaksarta*, Moscow, 1962.

VAN DEN BERGHE, L. *Archeologie de l'Iran Ancien*, Leiden, 1959.

ZADNEPROVSKII, YU. A. The Culture of the Early Farmers of Fergana, *MIA*, No. 118, 1962.

1

2

3

4

5

6

7

8

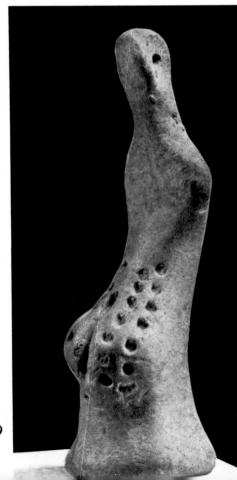

9

11

12

13

14

15

16

17

18

19

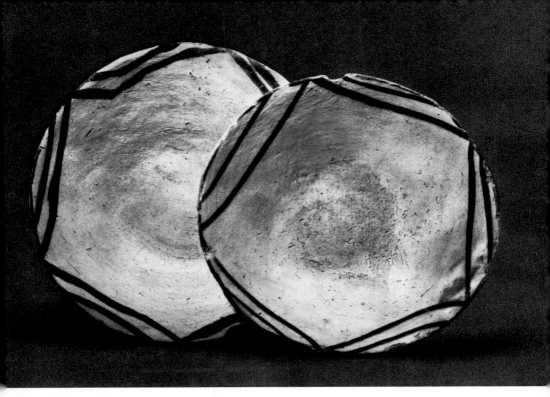

20

21

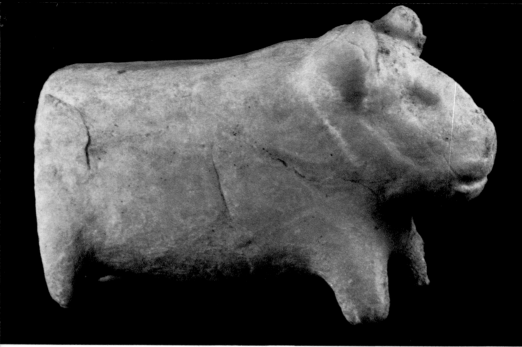

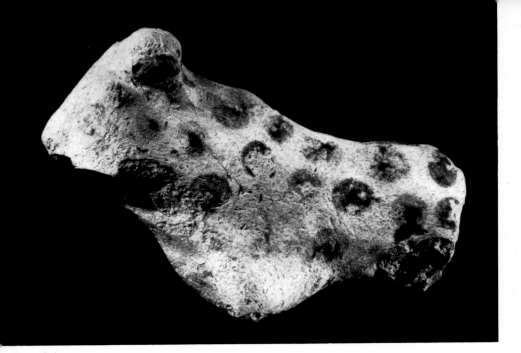

24

25

26

27

29

32

33

34

35

36

37

38

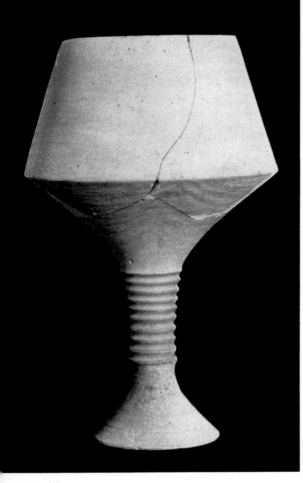

39

40

41

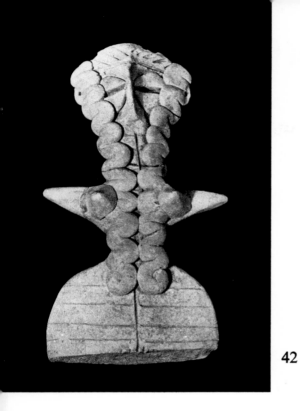

42

43

44

45

47

48

49

50

52

53

Notes on the Plates

213

Notes on the Plates

41 Clay figurines of the Namazga V period, from various sites

42 Female figurine from Altin-depe; Namazga V period

43 Altin-depe: figurine from a burial chamber; Namazga V period

44 Head of a figurine of the Namazga V period, from Altin-depe

45 Fragment of a clay plaque with incised signs; Altin-depe, Namazga V period

46, 47 Stone, metal and clay seals of the Namazga V period from southern Turkmenia. 46, Altin-depe; 47, Namazga-depe

48 General view of the excavations at Altin-depe. A house with fortifications is visible in the background

49, 50 Auchin-depe: pottery and beads of the Namazga VI period

51 Painted pottery of Yaz I type from Ulug-depe

52 Tagisken; general view of the cemetery

53 Excavations of the mausoleum at Tagisken

Index